79p

SCIENCE IN OUR WORLD

PRESENTING INFORMATION

Contributory Author
Brian Knapp, BSc, PhD
Art Director
Duncan McCrae, BSc
Special scientific models
Tim Fulford, MA, Head of Design and Technology,
Leighton Park School
Editorial consultants
Rita Owen, BSc and Sarah George, BEd
Special photography
Ian Gledhill
Illustrations
David Woodroffe
Science advisor
Jack Brettle, BSc, PhD,
Chief Research Scientist, Pilkington plc
Print consultants
Landmark Production Consultants Ltd
Printed and bound in Hong Kong
Produced by
EARTHSCAPE EDITIONS

First published in the United Kingdom in 1993
by Atlantic Europe Publishing Company Limited,
86 Peppard Road, Sonning Common, Reading,
Berkshire, RG4 9RP, UK
Telephone 0734 723751; Fax 0734 724488

Publication Data
Knapp, Brian
Presenting information – (Science in our world; 29)
1. Science – For children
2. Technology – For children
I. Title   II. Series
507

ISBN 1-869860-23-3

Acknowledgements
The publishers would like to thank the following:
Leighton Park School, Pilkington plc, Micklands
County Primary, Redlands County Primary School
and Volvo Henley Ag.

Picture credits
t=top b=bottom l=left r=right
All photographs are from the
Earthscape Editions library.

In this book you will find some words that have been shown in **bold** type. There is a full explanation of each of these words on pages 46 and 47.

Experiments that you might like to try for yourself have been put in a yellow box like this.

Contents

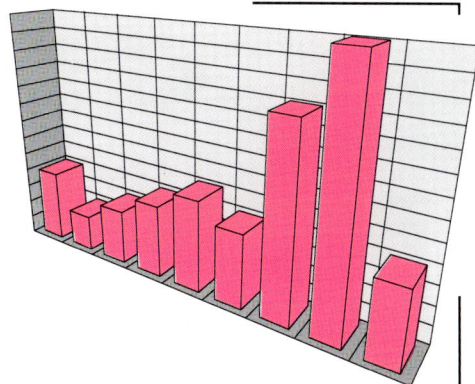

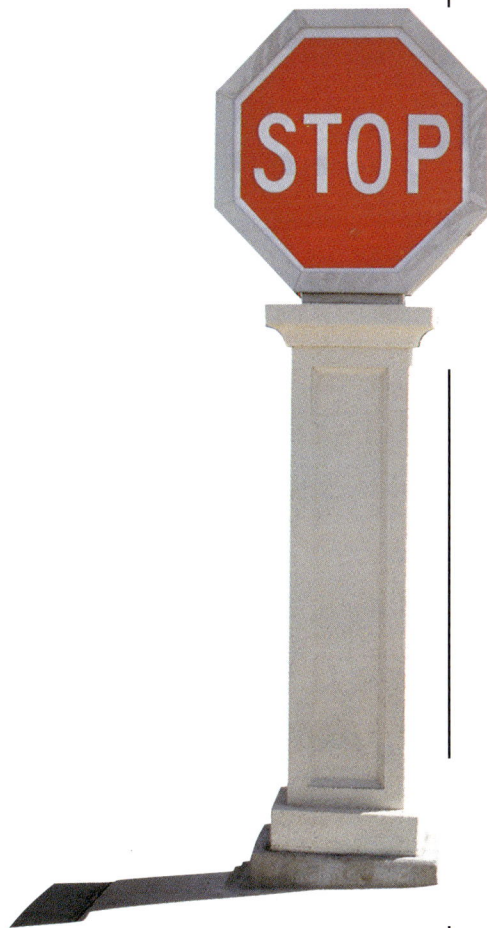

Introduction

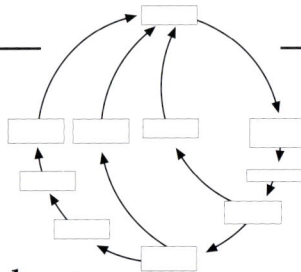

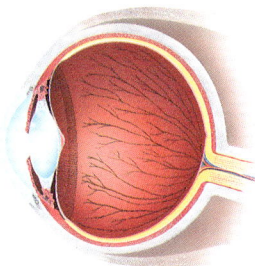

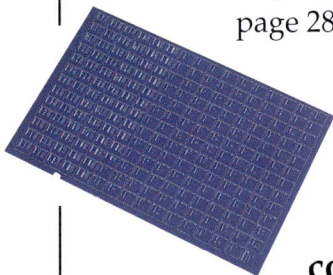

Lift up your arm and wave to someone. This is just one of the many ways that you can share information, that is communicate. Science can help us to understand how our world works *and* help us to share that knowledge freely with everyone else.

By sharing information, scientists enable **designers** and **technologists** to turn inventions into things for everyone to use. For example, radio and television now provide news and stories to billions of people across the world.

As you experiment with science there are many discoveries that you will make. The discoveries are made more fun if the results can be shared. The way to share information of all kinds – science, art, entertainment, news – is to present it clearly, and for this we have to understand how people see the world around them and how they learn.

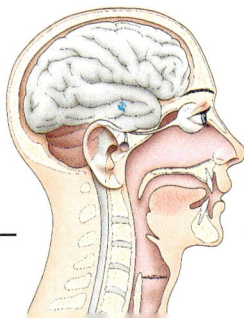

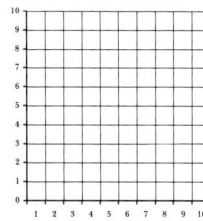

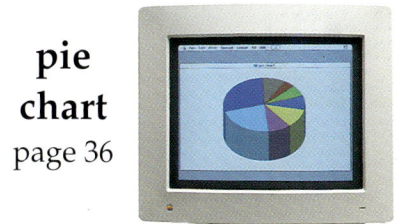

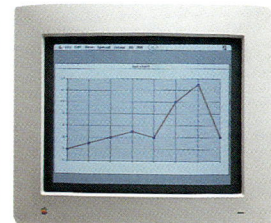

Sharing information is not new – cave dwellers thousands of years ago, for example, **communicated** with each other through drawing pictures. But the methods have changed. On our television screens today there are many colourful and exciting ways of presenting information using the special effects that computers can provide.

Simple messages are called signals. In the days before radio, for example, ships used flags hoisted high on the masts to send messages to others within a fleet. But the more complicated the message, or the more clearly it must stand out from the surroundings, the more we need to know about how the eye and the brain receive information.

Start to find out about the ways of presenting information in any way you choose. Just turn to a page to begin your discoveries.

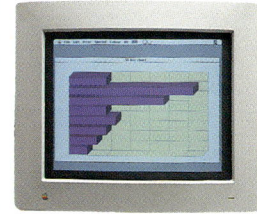

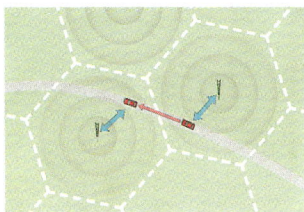

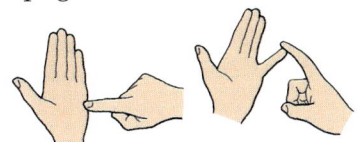

How we share information

Communicating is the way information is shared. Whether the communicating is by two people speaking, a person reading a book or a television **transmitter** sending signals to millions of TV sets, the process is basically the same. Here, as an example, are the stages of communicating by sound.

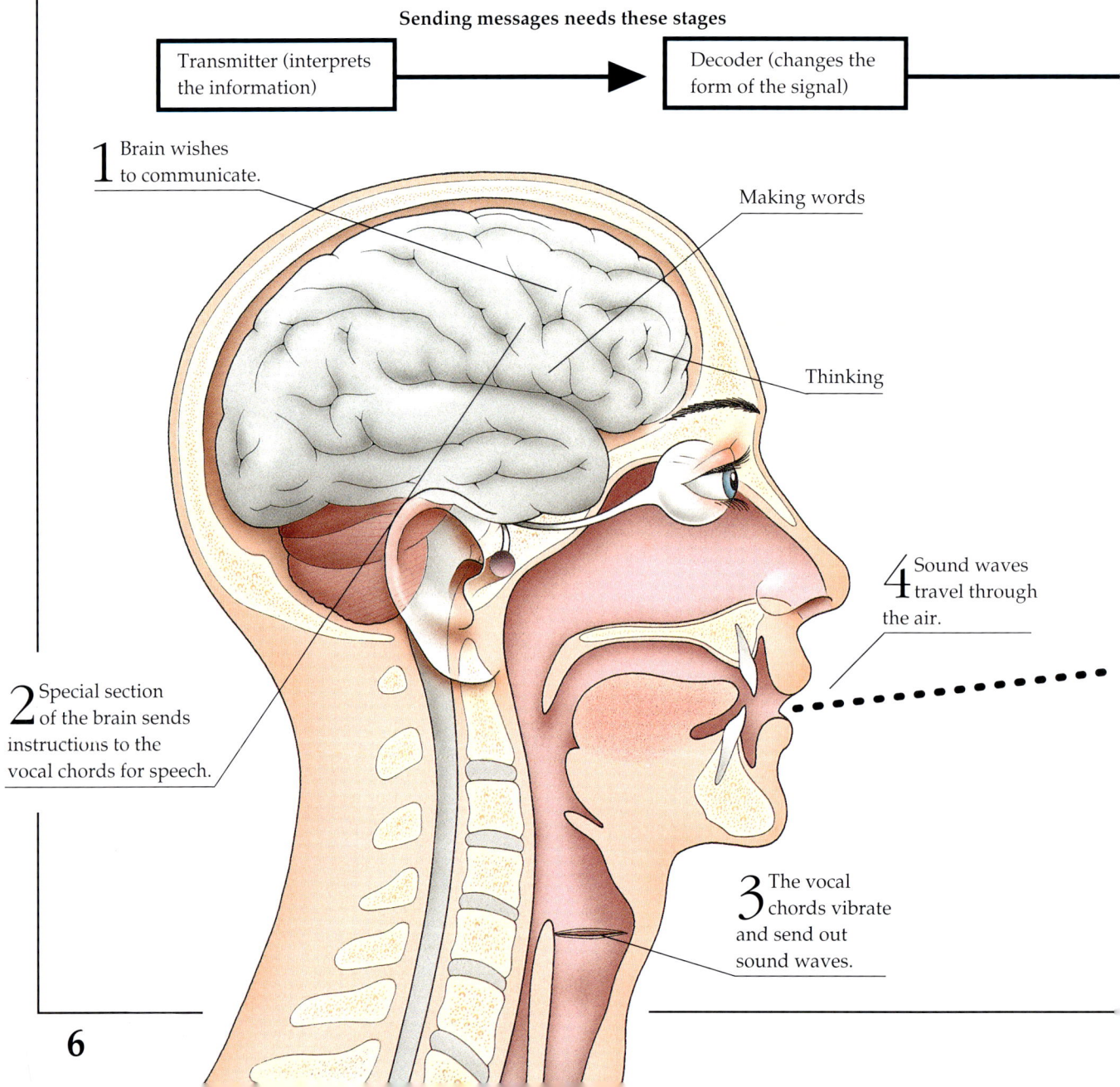

Sending messages needs these stages

| Transmitter (interprets the information) | → | Decoder (changes the form of the signal) |

1 Brain wishes to communicate.

Making words

Thinking

2 Special section of the brain sends instructions to the vocal chords for speech.

4 Sound waves travel through the air.

3 The vocal chords vibrate and send out sound waves.

Stages of communicating

There are several steps involved in sending and receiving messages by sound. For example, if we want to share an idea our brain has to send a message to our vocal chords to speak in a special pattern of sounds called language. This message travels though the air until it reaches the listener's eardrum. Here the sounds are converted into electrical signals that the listener's brain can understand.

When people communicate by telephone the message passes through more stages because sound waves have to be converted into radio waves by the handset.

Communicating by sight

Work out the stages in communicating needed when two people recognise each other in the street. Draw the stages on a tracing of the diagrams below.

Receiving messages needs these stages

Decoder (changes the form of the signal) → Receiver (interprets the information)

Hearing words

5 Sound received by ear drum.

6 Sound vibrations are converted to electrical signals by nerve cells.

7 Special section of the brain interprets information.

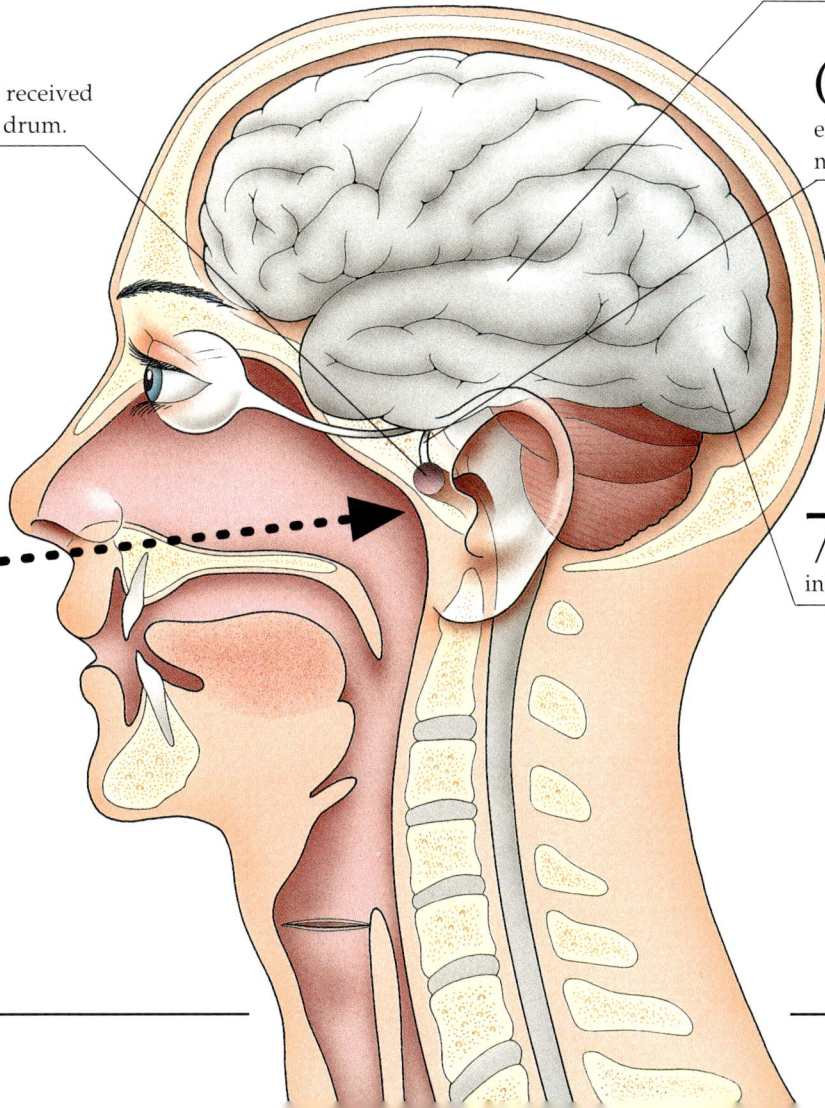

Person to person

Each of our senses – hearing, sight, touch, smell, and taste – is able to pick up signals sent by other people and the environment. Here are examples of how various senses are used in communication.

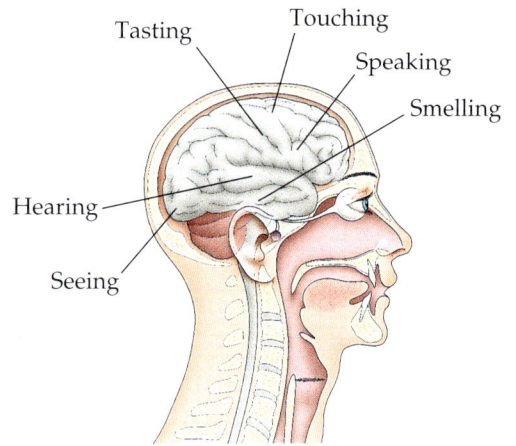

Tasting
Touching
Speaking
Smelling
Hearing
Seeing

Scared

These facial signs tell you much about the person's mood and needs. Notice how many changes there are between expressions.

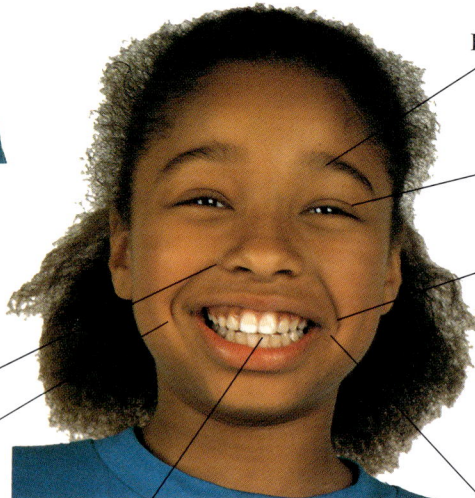

Height of eyebrows

Openness of eyes

Length of smile

Openness of nostrils and lines on bridge of nose

Lines on face

Direction of the end of the mouth

Openness of the mouth

Smiling

Sad

Bored

(For more information on senses see the book Senses *in the* Science in our world *series.)*

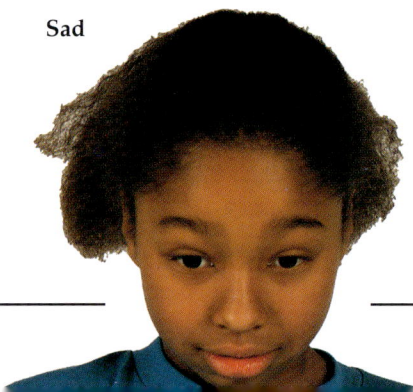

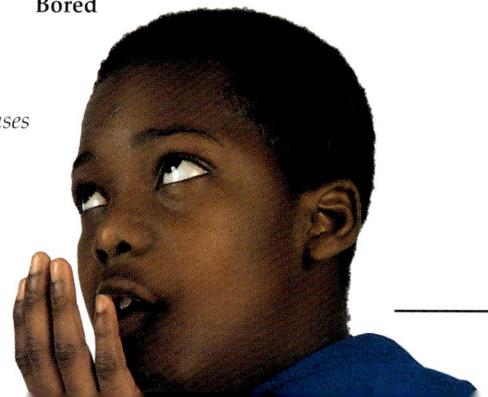

Semaphore

This ancient system of signals (using flags or flashing lights) allows messages to be sent between two people who are within sight of each other.

Flashing lights semaphore is still used by navies when ships are close together and they want to maintain radio silence, for example when they are close to, but just out of sight of, an enemy.

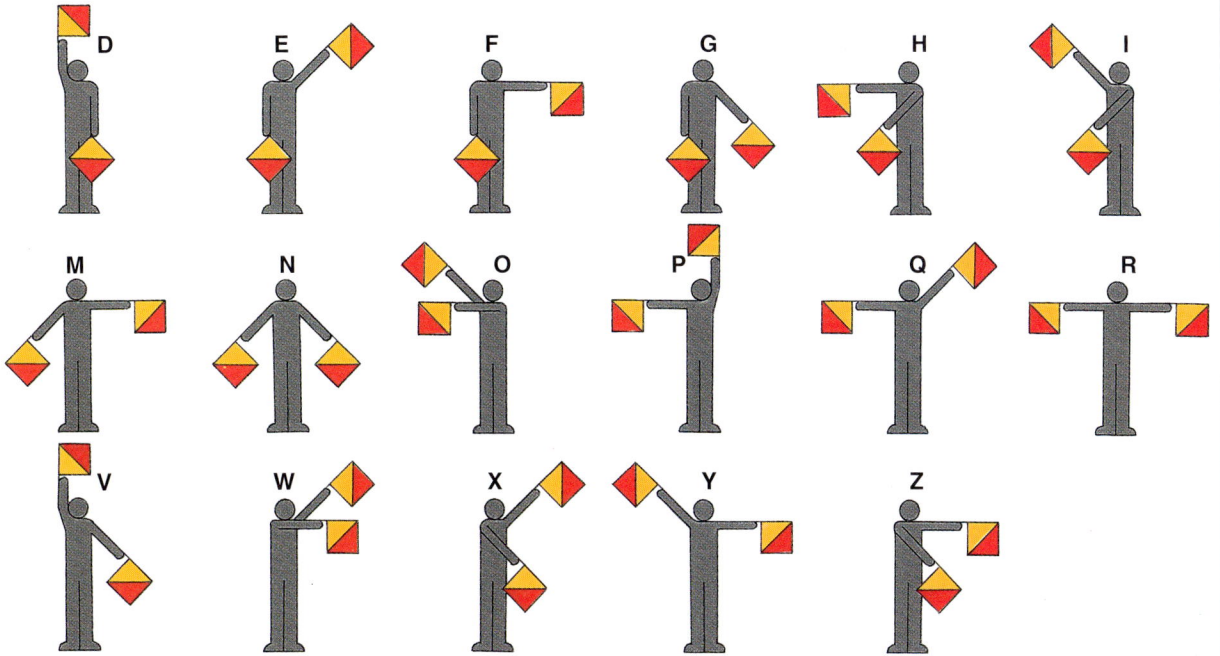

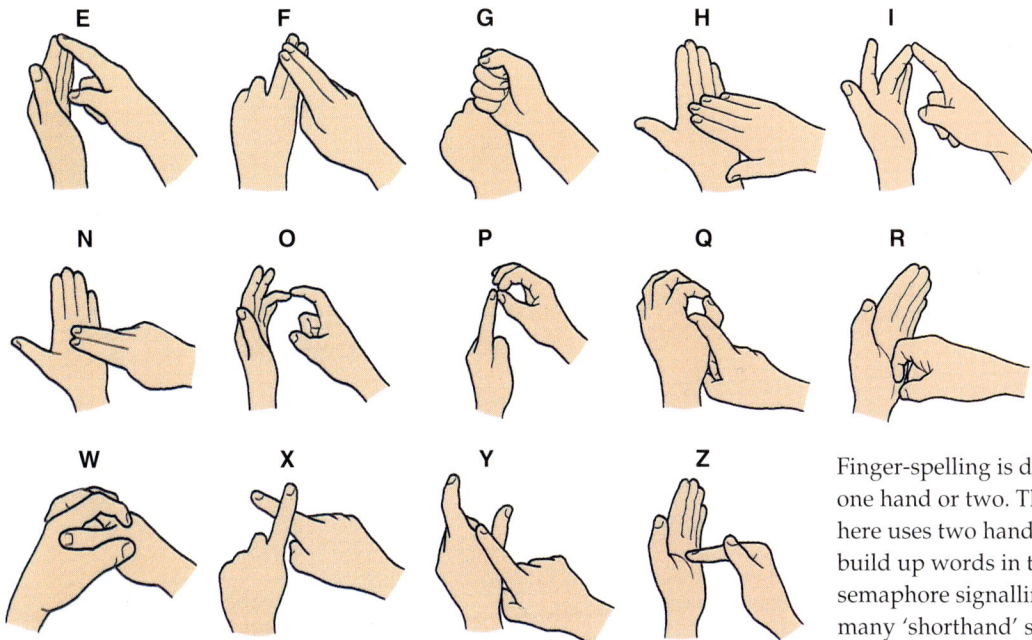

Finger-spelling is done with either one hand or two. The system shown here uses two hands. It is used to build up words in the same way as semaphore signalling, but there are many 'shorthand' signals used for common words as well.

In focus

The eye is well adapted to receive information in an economical way. The whole area we can see is called the **field of view** but the most important region of sight is near the centre.

Our eyes always try to get the centre of the field of view in **focus** because it is here that we can receive the maximum amount of information.

Knowing that there is a small field of focused vision is very important for presenting all kinds of information.

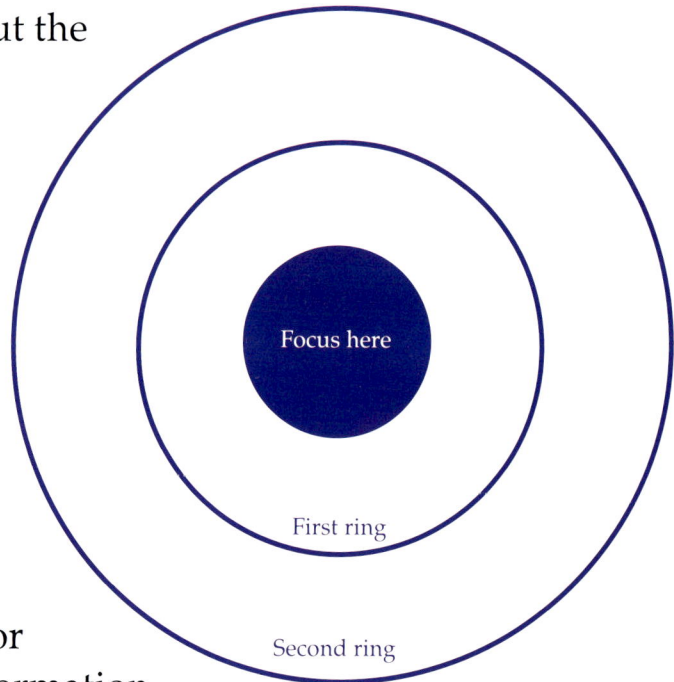

Focus here

First ring

Second ring

Test your field of focused vision
Look at the diagram above and focus on the words 'Focus here'. While keeping focused on the centre, try to gauge how far from the 'bulls-eye' appears in focus. Can you read the word 'First ring' or 'Second ring'? The chances are you can not.

Repeat the test while typing on a computer keyboard. Focus on the letter G. How many other letters and numbers are in focus?

1 Find out if this line of writing is too long. Do you have to turn your head a lot to follow the words along the line or can you manage conveniently? Stare at the middle and find out how many words are in focus.

2 Find out if this line of writing is too long. Do you have to turn your head a lot to follow

Only things within 2 ° (degrees) of the centre of the eye are truly in focus.

Regions to the side of the field of view do not have to be in focus. They are used to tell us about the size of an object and the way it is moving.

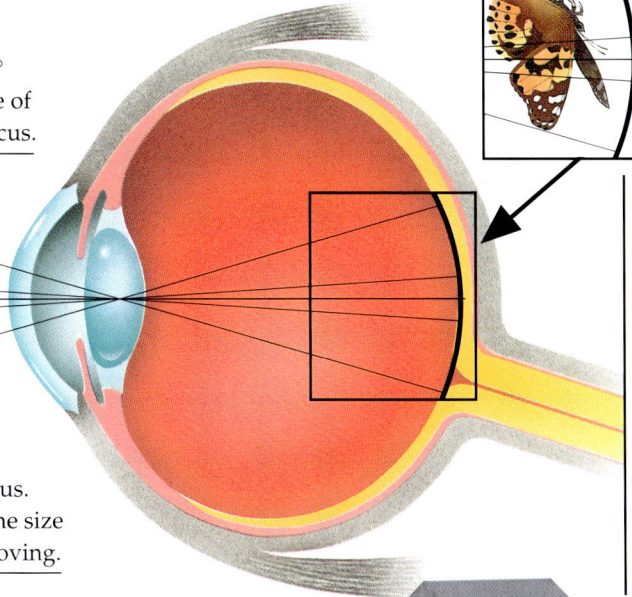

Design a symbol

Design a symbol that can be seen by people passing through a classroom door to warn them that people pushing trolleys of school dinners might be using the corridor beyond, so they should therefore leave the classroom slowly.

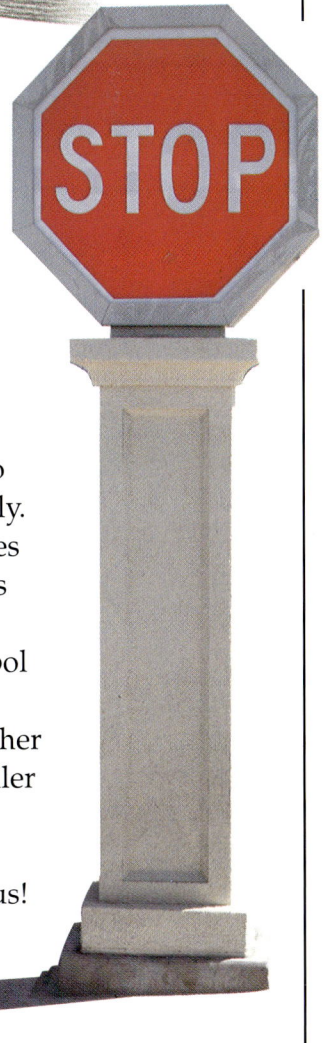

PLEASE BE CAREFUL BECAUSE THE JUNCTION AHEAD MAY BE DANGEROUS IF YOU APPROACH IT TOO QUICKLY.

STOP

Safety road signs

Road signs often have to be read quickly and the eye therefore also has to scan across the signs rapidly.

Remember that only two degrees are in focus, so reading long signs will not be possible.

The brain will recognise a symbol much faster than a word. It is therefore safer to use symbols rather than words. Symbols can be smaller and be seen from farther away, because they can be recognised even if they do not appear in focus!

the words along the line? Stare at the middle and find out how many words are in focus.

Using colour

Colour gives us an enormous amount of extra information about our world. Our brain recognises and uses colours in special ways and any information that we want to share needs to be carefully designed for greatest effect.

By highlighting the important parts of a model with different colours it is much easier to see how it works.

(For more information on how this pendulum works see the book Time *in the Science in our world series.)*

Traffic lights are partly designed to be interpreted by people who have red-green colour blindness.

Colour codes

The sign above gives information about the restrictions for vehicles in the historical district (centro storico) of Verona, an Italian city. Colour has been used to give additional information. The red is used on instruction signs (no waiting – lower left, no parking – lower right). Colour coding has been used to make other important information clear. What do (i) the sign showing two people in a blue circle; (ii) the blue curved line; and (iii) the yellow area mean?

Colour blindness

Some people have a condition known as **colour blindness**. This means that they cannot easily tell the difference between two colours such as red and green. So, for example, although it is possible to make a single traffic light change through the colours red, then amber and then green, a colour blind person could not tell these colours apart and therefore not know when to stop and when to go. Having three lights in a column gets over this problem.

It is similarly helpful if signs are not designed with red letters on a green background. By contrast, coloured letters on a white background and black letters on a coloured background can be seen by everyone.

Using colour sparingly

It is very tempting to use a lot of colour, but this can add confusion rather than make a message clear. Because the brain pays more attention to colour, designers use colour to highlight special information.

Study the picture above which shows part of a city street at night. What did you see first of all? See how many messages you can find in the picture.

Pattern and contrast

The brain 'collects' information to make sense of the world. Pattern and contrast are part of the shorthand that the brain uses to keep track of objects. For example, it is much easier to follow a black cat crossing a white background than a black cat on a dark brown background.

By noting just the edges of objects – where they change pattern or where there is a contrast of colour – the brain uses less computing power and can therefore react more quickly.

This picture has high contrast

This picture has normal contrast

Contrast, brightness and colour
We use contrast to find the edges to objects and colour to sort them out when the contrast is poor. Look at these three pictures. They are the same brightness but one has high contrast and the other low contrast. Which is easiest to see?

Your home TV set has brightness, colour and contrast controls on it. With the agreement of other people in your home, turn each of the controls in turn to see what effects they have.

This picture has low contrast

Military aircraft are painted with special colours and patterns to make them less visible to an enemy. They are often painted in wavy 'landscape' or 'ocean' colours on their upper side, and sky colours on their underside. This is the famous B52 bomber. From its camouflage colours can you guess what time of day this plane may have been used?

Patterns that fool the brain

The brain stores many patterns and when it sees a new object it uses the stored patterns for reference. This is the reason why, if the patterns are chosen carefully they can be made to fool the brain: an **illusion** has been created. For example, identical lines with arrow heads can be made to look different lengths as shown below.

Artists draw lines which meet at a point if they want to make the brain feel that a picture has depth (see also page 18).

Illusions can be used to make roads safer. For example the painted lines that help to mark the edges of some country roads can be drawn so that they make the brain think the road is getting narrower. This impression makes most drivers slow down.

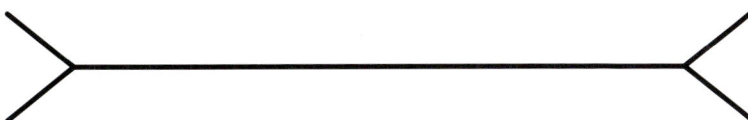

These lines are the same length, but the shapes on the ends confuse the brain in to thinking that one line is longer than the other.

Perspective

We live in a three **dimensional** world. However, we often have to represent our world on flat pieces of paper which only have two dimensions. We get over this problem by creating an illusion of depth. This is called drawing in perspective.

Find out about the need for perspective.
Trace each of these kitchen shapes and then place them on a piece of plain paper.

Arrange all the pieces until they appear to look as though they make a real kitchen.

Place a further piece of tracing paper over the kitchen shapes and trace off the lines of the edges. You will discover that they all go to a common vanishing point, showing that the brain and eye have remembered what the real world looks like and guided you as you placed your pieces on the paper.

Fit your tracing over the perspective grid shown on the right and prove they have a common vanishing point.

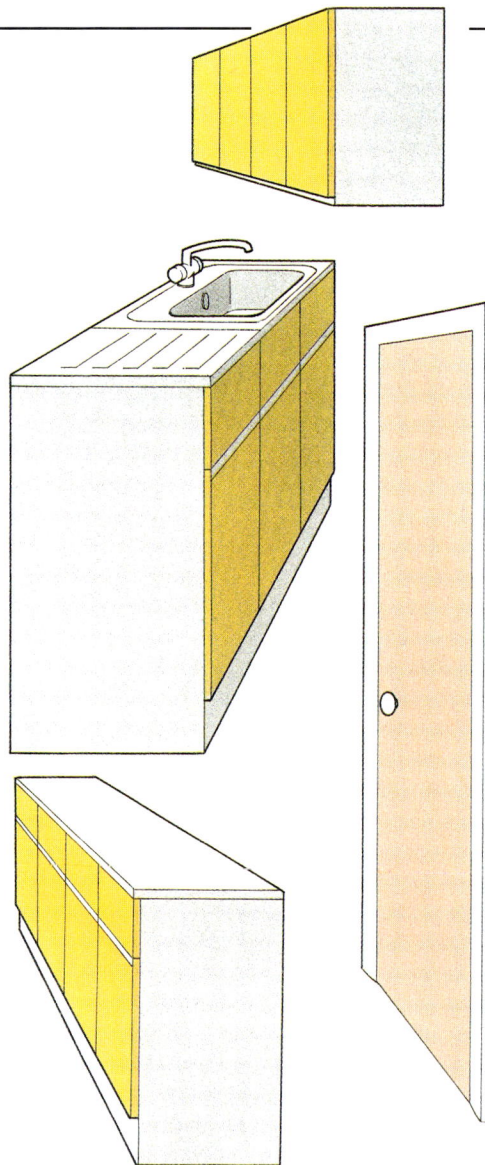

The eye is a simple **lens** – objects that are closer will appear bigger and those further away will seem smaller. The brain learns to judge distance by size in this way.

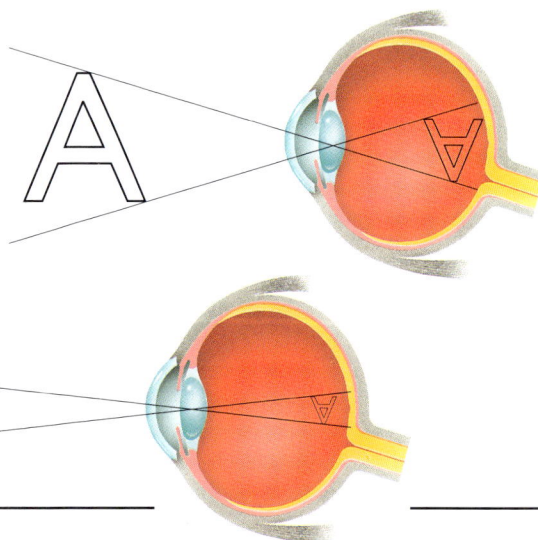

The perspective grid

The diagram above is called a perspective grid. The point where all the lines converge is called the vanishing point.

The perspective grid uses the property that objects appear smaller when they are farther away. It shows you that by drawing something small you can give the impression that it is far away.

This is a perspective grid. If you focus on the vanishing point the grid lines appear to make a three-dimensional corridor.

Symbols

With so many people moving around the world and so many languages spoken, it has become increasingly important for travellers to have some means of sharing information.

The range of internationally recognised symbols – **pictographs** – used today may look familiar, but it has been very difficult to find symbols that give the same message to people from all over the world.

Signs that imitate arms

Everyone uses their arms and hands to point out directions. It is the most easily understood international sign. So a signpost with an arm-like shape will be readily recognised as a signpost.

An arrow is a traditional symbol and so will be readily understood all over the world. Other clear signs include people and common objects such as telephones.

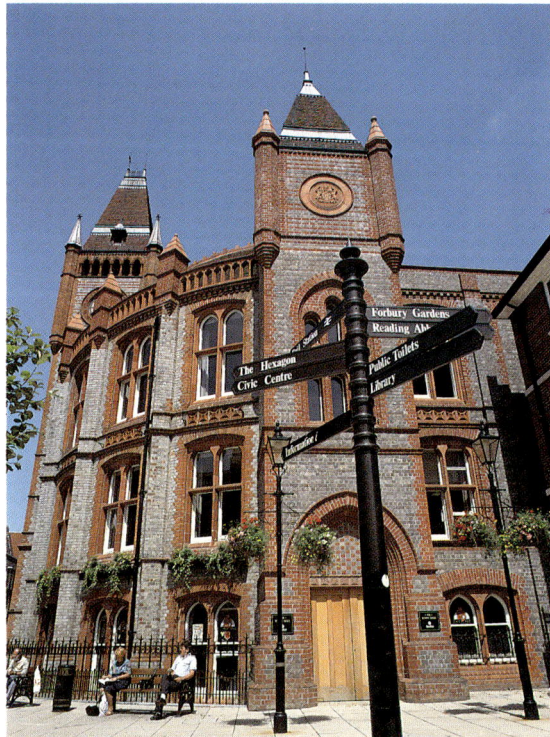

This black signpost is intended for people who are in the centre of a town. It is meant for people unfamiliar with the town, but who speak the national language. As a result no attempt has been made to make the signs international.

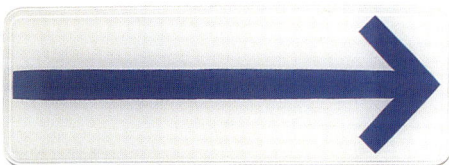

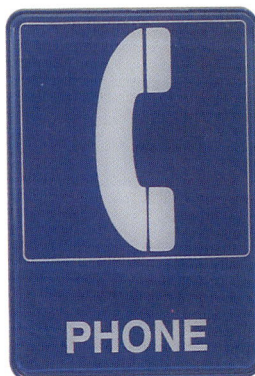

PHONE

DANGER MINE SHAFTS

The sign above is meant to be useful to foreigners as well as local people and it has been placed in a tourist area which was once a tin mine. The red triangle is an international symbol for danger. It means 'this board is a signpost about danger'.

Having noticed the signpost a foreigner can then concentrate on understanding the exact words below the symbol. Without the symbol someone who did not read English might not appreciate the danger.

DANGER MINE SHAFTS

21

Getting the size right

Have you ever wondered why so many signs are difficult to read? Part of the difficulty is often caused by the sign being the wrong size.

To understand what size the writing should be you need to know how the eye works.

What the lens does

The lens of the eye turns an image upside down and then focuses it on the area of sensitive cells at the back of the eye.

In the diagrams on the right two lines have been drawn to show the way a ray of light from the top and bottom of a letter 'A' each reach the eye. You can see that, for the A to appear to be the same size in each case, the more distant letter must be larger. If it is twice as far away it must be twice the height and so on.

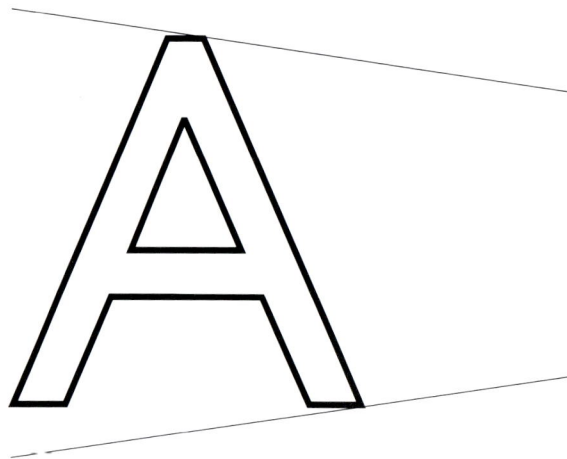

Work out how big lettering should be

Suppose you were to make a sign that showed arrivals and departures for use in a railway station. Imagine that people are likely to stand about 30 m from the sign. How big should the lettering be?

Start with the lettering below and measure its height. Now hold it away from you until you can no longer read it. Bring it slightly closer until you can read it again and measure this distance.

Now divide the distance you have measured into the distance the real sign will be seen from. This tells you how much bigger to make the sign than the writing on the page.

For example, if you can read the word ARRIVALS (shown below) at 2 m and the real sign is to be read at 30 m then the real sign will be 30 m divided by 2 m, or 15 times farther away. This means that the size of the letters will also need to be 15 times larger than the size of the letters on the page.

Make a sign with letters this size and check that you can read it easily at 30 m.

ARRIVALS

In these two diagrams the image of the letter A projected onto the back of the eye is exactly the same size.

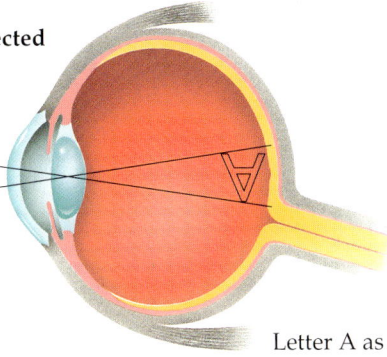

A

Letter A as it appears in the eye. The brain interprets the image so that it is seen 'the right way up'.

Light ray from the top of the letter A

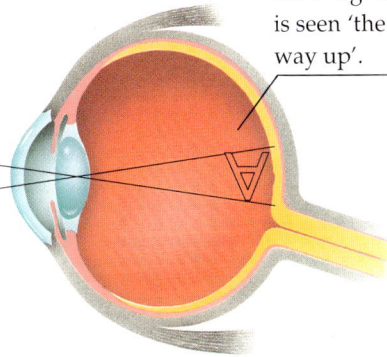

Light ray from the bottom of the letter A

The information on these TV monitors can be smaller than the information on a main station arrivals board because people are able to stand close to the monitors.

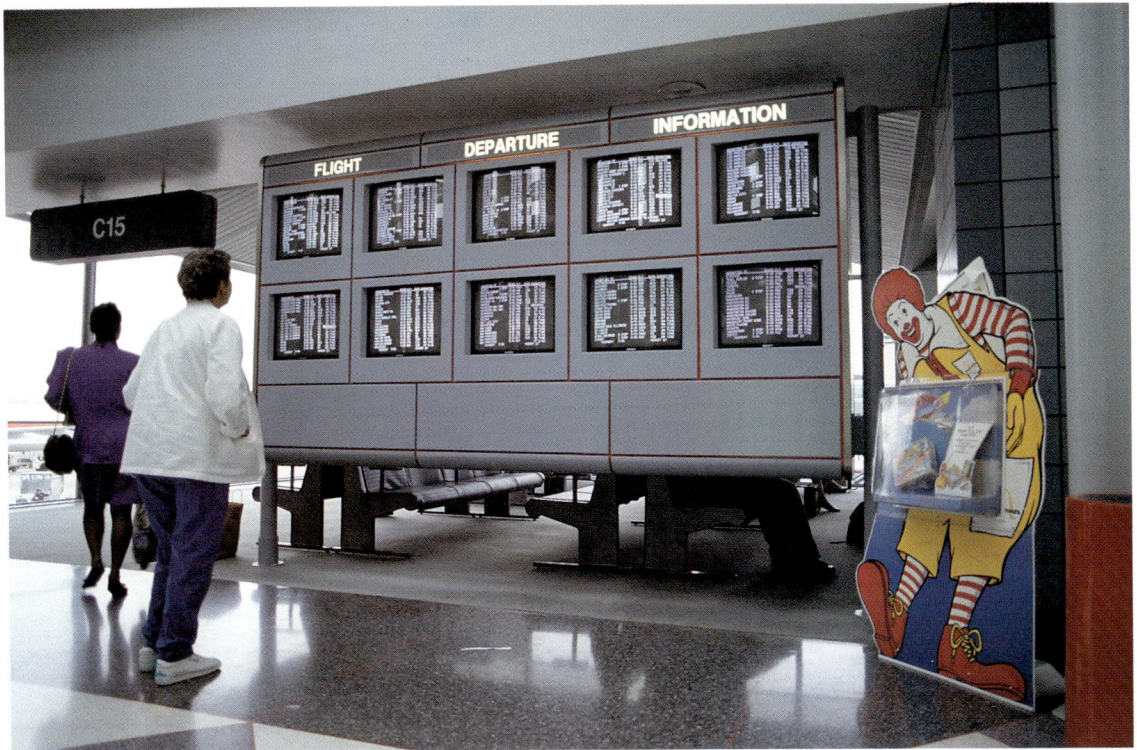

Understanding eyesight problems

Not everyone is fortunate enough to have really good eyesight (often called 20/20 vision). As a result, many people, and especially the old, find it harder to read and to see objects clearly.

This means that we need to think carefully about the way we present our information, so that these people don't miss out.

Design for those in need
The diagram on the opposite page shows a few of the problems that people may have with their sight and some of the simple things that can be done to make life easier for them.

It makes sense to design, wherever possible, for those with poorer eyesight rather than for those with perfect vision. In this way the most people possible are helped to enjoy their lives.

These two pictures show the kind of effect experienced by people who are 'long-sighted' (on the right) and those who are 'short-sighted' (above).

Long-sighted people would not be able to focus on the flowers in the foreground and they will appear blurred; short-sighted people would see the flowers clearly but the building in the background would remain blurred.

Problem:
About three times the light level is needed to read when you are old than when you are young
Remedy:
Make sure reading lights are very bright – use new fluorescent lamps to keep the cost of good lighting low.

Problem:
The eye muscles are weaker and they cannot make the lens change shape enough to see things that are close up.
Remedy:
make signs big enough to be read at more than 60 cm.

The image is focused on retina.

These muscles stretch the lens to focus.

Rods and cones identify colour.

These fibres connect the muscles to the lens.

Blind spot

Lens

Optic nerve

Cornea

Conjunctiva protects surface of cornea.

Problem:
The lens becomes thicker and scatters the light, so direct lights appear to glare.
Remedy:
Do not use harsh direct lights such as unshielded fluorescent tubes.

Fluids of the eye

Problem:
The lens and fluids in the eye become slightly more yellow. This means that blue and green are hard to see and dark colours can all seem to be black.
Remedy:
Make sure important signs are in red.

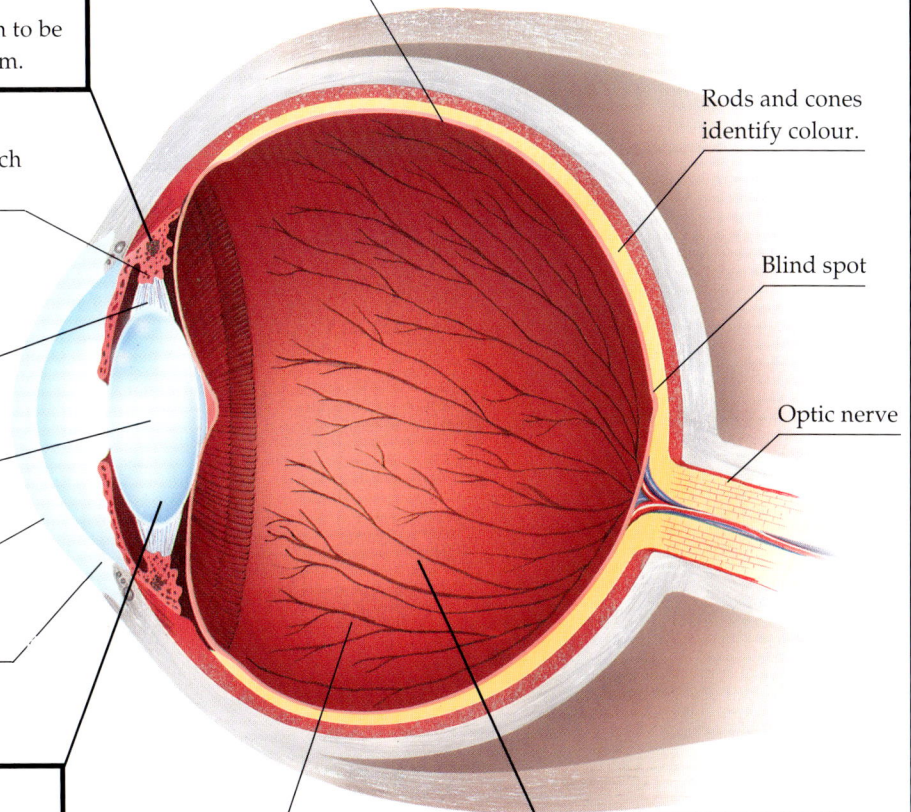

Scientifically designed logos

A logo is a symbol that is easily recognised. It has been discovered that people generally pick out and remember simple designs better than words, and so many companies now use symbols as a means of easy recognition. When symbols are used in this way they are called logos.

To be most effective a logo should make use of the science described on the previous pages. Here is a way of testing how scientifically they have been designed.

Test out logos
Use the set of scientific rules shown on the right to test the logos shown in the street scene below. Apply all five rules to each message shown in the street scene and decide whether they meet all the needs. Sketch out any improvements you think could be made to the logos that seem least clear to you.

Science rules for logos

1. It must be easily recognised by its shape, its simple design and its colour.
2. It must not cause difficulties for colour-blind people.
3. It must be large enough to be seen in the place where it is used; the faster people are moving, the bigger it must be.
4. It must be easy for people to recognise no matter what language they speak.
5. It must have good contrast with the background wherever it is used.

Design a logo

Design, or, if you have one, redesign a logo for your school or club. First you must think of a design that reflects the message you want to give. Then apply the rules of science for logos to adjust the design for maximum impact.

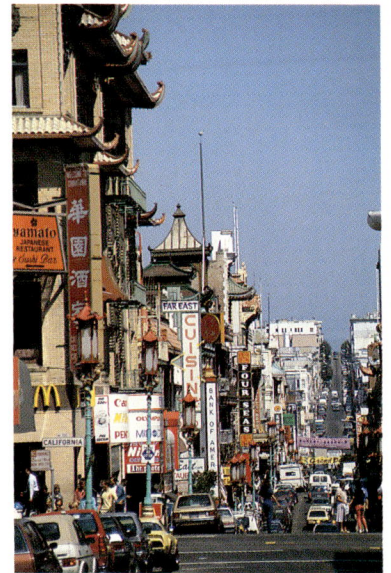

These signs are not meant to be read at a glance. However, even a person walking along would have problems because there are no logos to help.

27

Saving space

When people are handling large amounts of information, such as when they are looking through back numbers of newspapers or population records for history and geography projects, it is often convenient to be able to scan quickly rather than turn over the pages of the original materials.

To provide for rapid scanning, many sources of information are now reduced and kept as photographic film, or they are transferred to computer disks.

The original size of pages in this series.

Cameras, projectors and microscopes

A camera is a device for reducing the size of the real world onto a small photographic plate.

The lens in a camera works in the same way as the lens in a human eye. This means that, for example, a whole page of a book can be made as small as needed, if necessary even smaller than a full stop.

A microscope and a projector work like a camera in reverse, making small objects (such as photographic transparencies) appear large. A projector used to read information is often called a microfiche reader.

To read the miniature information the lens is used to magnify, just as it is in a microscope. A strong beam of light is shone through the film and the lens used to focus the image onto a screen.

This is part of a set of microfiche cards used by a motor repair workshop. Thousands of part references are kept on several small sheets which can easily be seen through a microfiche reader.

Microfiche cards
You will find film readers (often called microfiche-readers) in libraries. Ask a librarian to show you how a microfiche reader works and what it is used for.

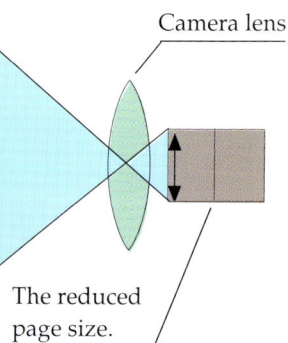

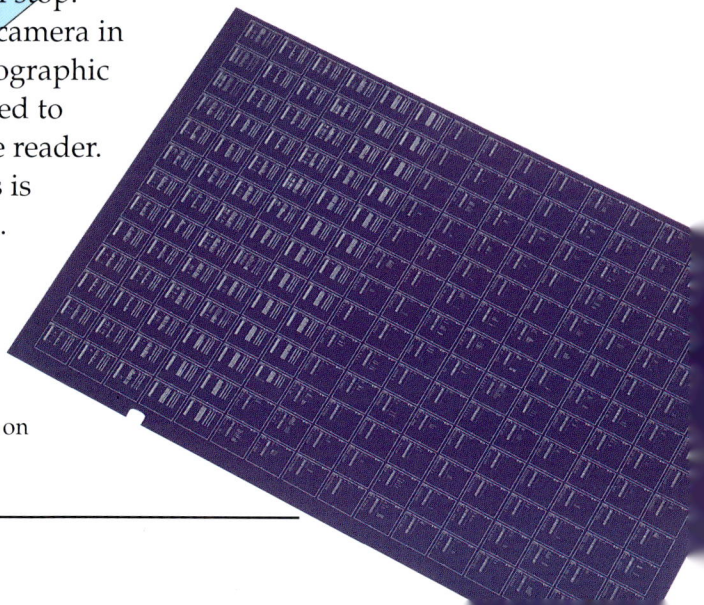

Camera lens

The reduced page size.

Computer storage

Pictures and text can be stored on computer **magnetic disk**s or **optical discs** just like the CDs you use for music.

The computer can rapidly search for any item by title or word: a task that might otherwise take a reader hours of toil.

(For more information on computers and data storage see the book Computers and Robots *in the Science in our world series.)*

The information in this stack of encyclopedias has been placed on to a single compact disc. The disc is read by a computer. Any part of the encyclopedia can be selected and displayed on the screen in a few seconds. The disc also has room for sound effects and so stores even more information than the encyclopedias.

Your own film archive

Use a camera with a transparency film to take photographs of pages in a newspaper or magazine.

If you experiment with a zoom lens on the camera you may be able to get many pages of a newspaper onto the same transparency.

Then get the film developed and mounted. The slides can then be shown through a school or home projector.

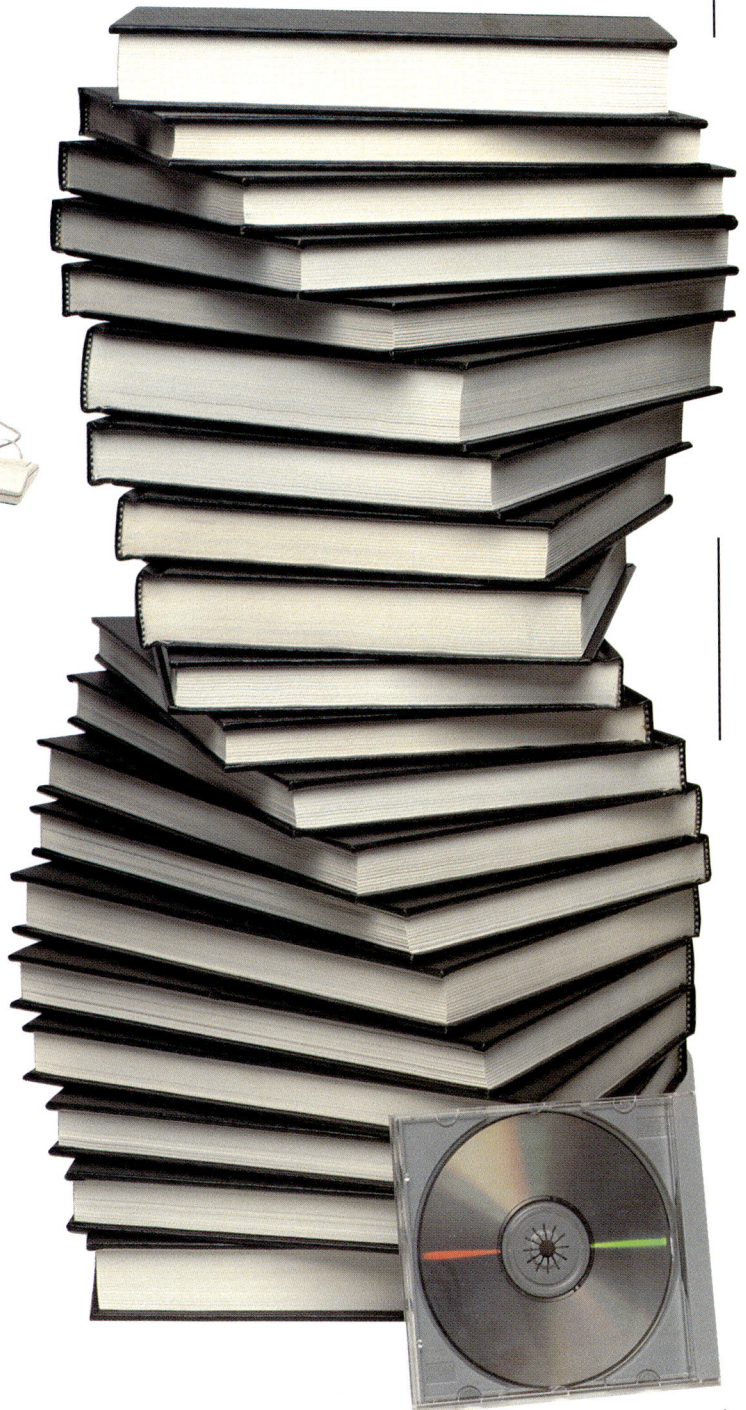

Presenting scientific information

In the first part of this book we have discussed the way science can explain how we see information and how to store information conveniently. This knowledge has helped designers and manufacturers to produce things that are easier, more attractive and safer both to use and understand.

The results of your experiments can also be made attractive and easy to understand by using charts.

These charts have all been produced by computer. Most computers will produce charts swiftly and accurately.

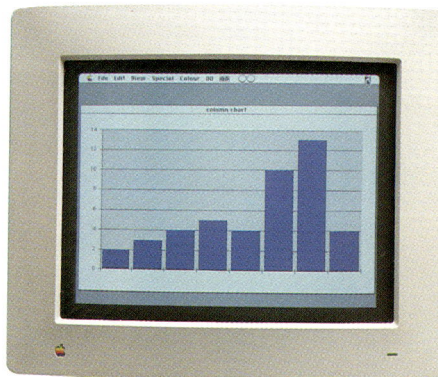

Column chart

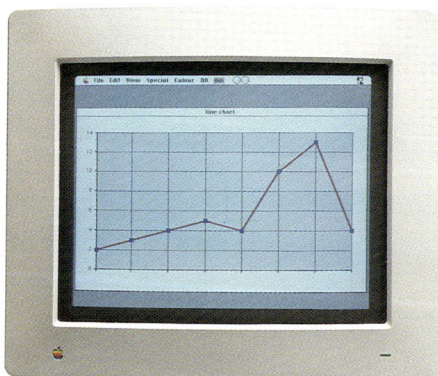

Line chart

Presenting the results of investigations
There are usually many ways to present the results of an investigation. Remember that there are three things to consider: (a) be accurate, (b) present material at a size that is easy to read, and (c) make the results look attractive by the use of colour, design and pattern.

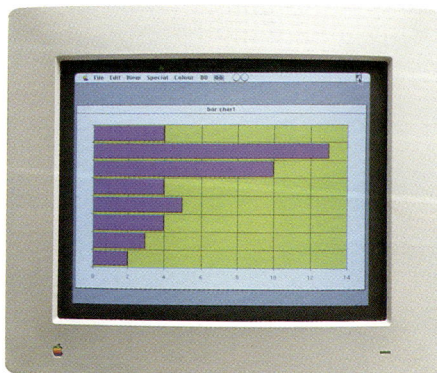

Bar chart

Pie chart

A chart

When you investigate a problem you will often make many measurements. This is referred to as your **data**.

   If the amount of data is very large the information you have gathered can be difficult to understand. Charts can often help to make presentation easier.

Axes and scales

All charts are drawn accurately to size (scale). The **axes** are lines on which the scales are drawn.

   If we were measuring people in a class one axis would be scaled for height, and the other axis would be numbers having the same height. It is important to label each axis clearly.

The chart on the right has clearly labelled axes and a grid of lines to make it easier to plot values. The horizontal axis has been drawn for a column chart (see page 32). An axis for a line chart of shown on page 38. Squared paper can be used to provide a ready-made grid.

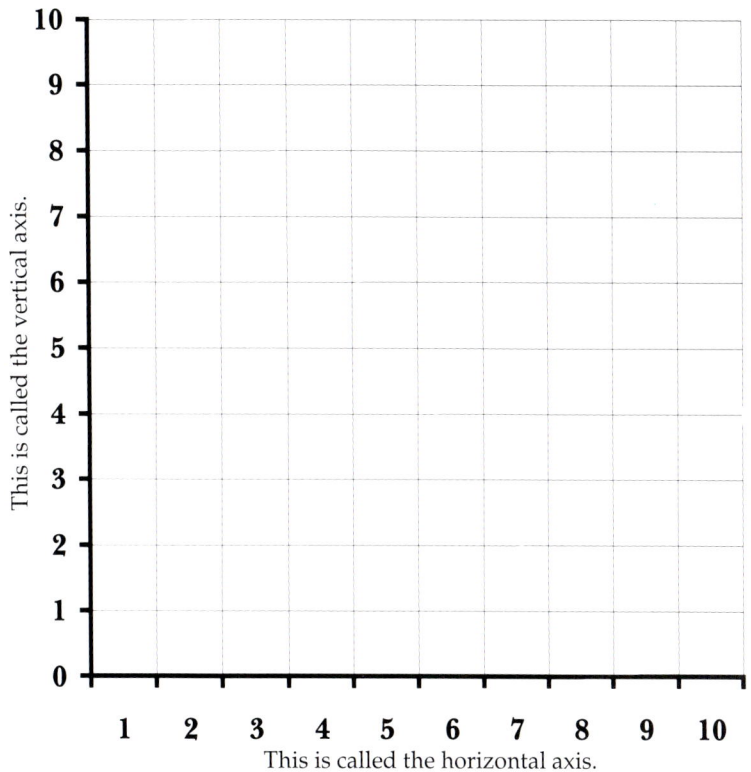

This is called the vertical axis.

This is called the horizontal axis.

DATA FOR THE GRAPHIC PRESENTATIONS ON PAGES 32 TO 41

Compute your data

The charts shown on the following pages all use the same information, which is shown here. This allows you to see how the same information can be presented in many different ways depending on what your purpose is. You could think of it as rainfall in each month, the number of people in height bands, or the number of drops from a tap each second.

   If your computer has a chart program, feed these data into the program and see if you can get the same charts as the ones shown on these pages.

| 4 | 2 | 3 | 4 | 5 | 4 | 10 | 13 | 4 |

Column charts

One of the easiest ways of presenting information is with a column chart. A column chart needs two sets of information: category (for example time period such as months) and the size of the category (for example the amount of rain that fell in each month).

DATA									
Months of the year	Jan.	Feb.	Mar.	Apr.	May	June	July	Aug.	Sept.
Rainfall (millimetres)	4	2	3	4	5	4	10	13	4

2 Then split each axis into a number of even divisions and add numbers to make a scale. If you are making a rainfall chart, months are set out on the horizontal axis and rainfall totals on the vertical axis (scale in mm).

1 Make a column chart by first drawing two lines (axes) at right angles.

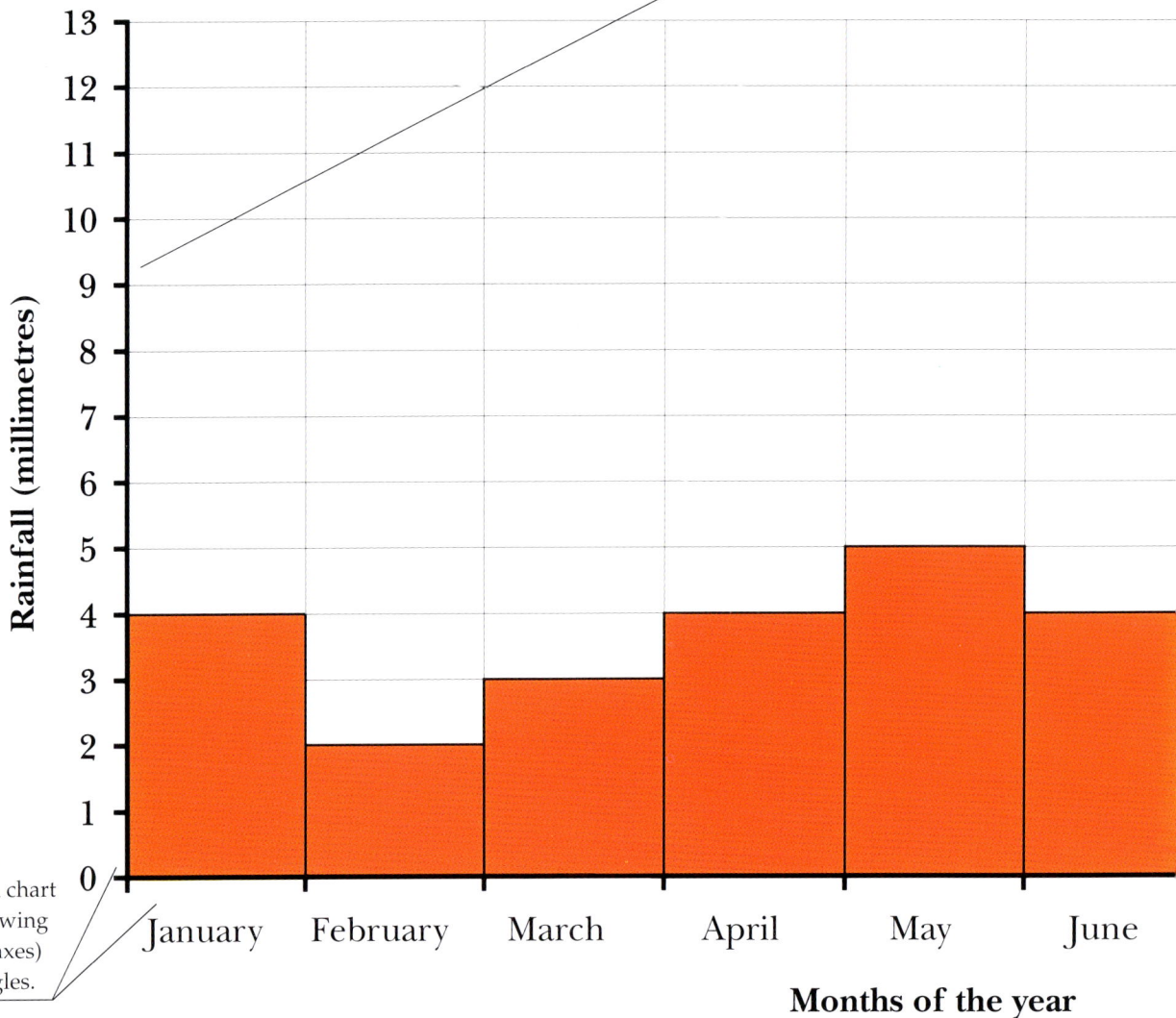

Rainfall (millimetres) (vertical axis, 0 to 13)

January, February, March, April, May, June (horizontal axis)

Months of the year

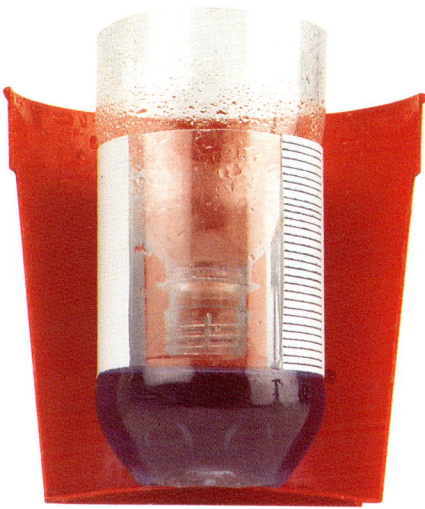

This is a simple raingauge: For more information on measuring rain see the books *Weather* and *Measuring* in the Science in our world series.

(For more examples on using column charts see the book Science and Design *in the* Science in our world series.)

Class heights
Measure the heights of people in your class and group them into categories of 10 mm. Plot these results as a column chart using the method shown here.

The picture above shows a quadrat. You could show the results of a survey across a field using a quadrat by means of a column chart. Each place on the survey might be measured with a quadrat and the total number of different plants (species) recorded. These totals are then set out as columns (vertical axis) against distance (horizontal axis).

For more information on measuring the species in an area see the book *Measuring* in the Science in our world series.

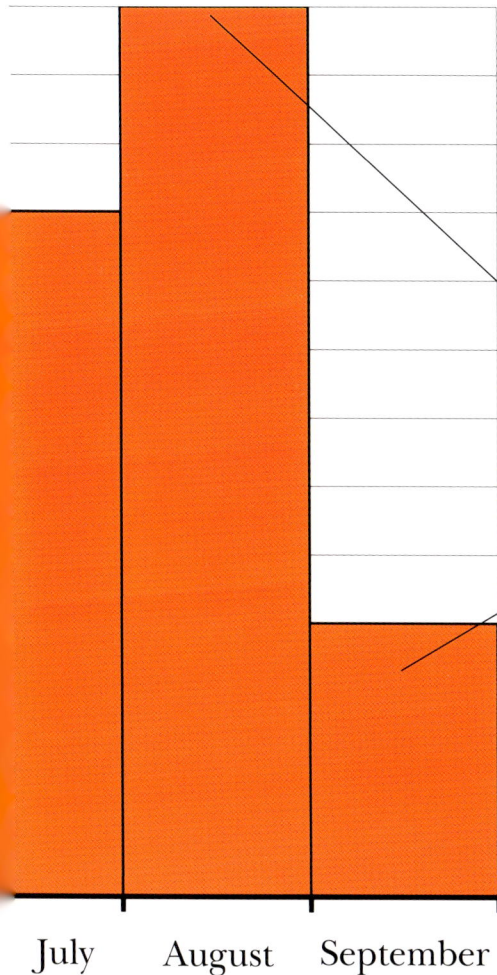

3 Each number from the data is now drawn as a column. If rainfall in August was 13 mm, a column is drawn for the month of August until it reaches the 13 mm level on the chart.

4 The columns are then coloured in.

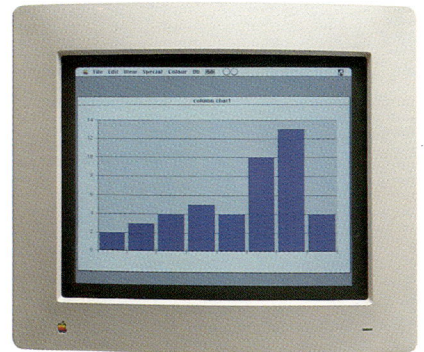

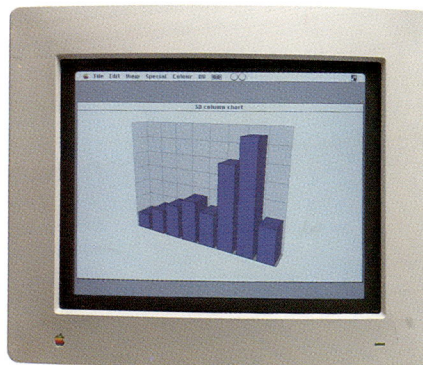

A computer will make up column charts at the touch of a button. Many computers will show your results as a 3D (three-dimensional) column chart.

July   August   September

Bar charts

A bar chart is a column chart with the columns lying on their side. It may be used when showing, for example, the time it took for several competitors to complete a task. Each of the competitors is shown as a bar, the time they took is shown by the length of the bar.

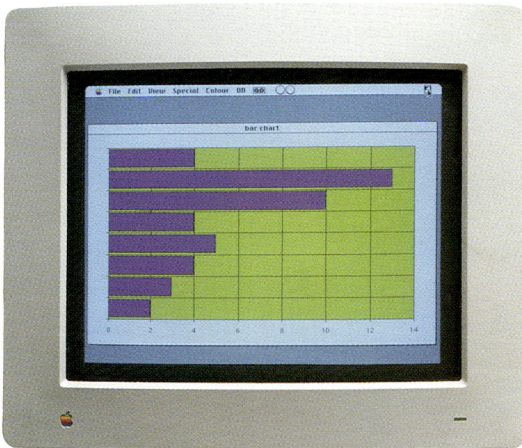

A computer will make up bar charts at the touch of a button.

1 Make a bar chart by first drawing two lines (axes) at right angles.

2 Then split each axis into a number of even divisions and add numbers to make a scale. If you are making a chart that uses time, seconds are set out on the horizontal axis and competitors results on the vertical axis (scale given as names: Anna, Sandip etc.).

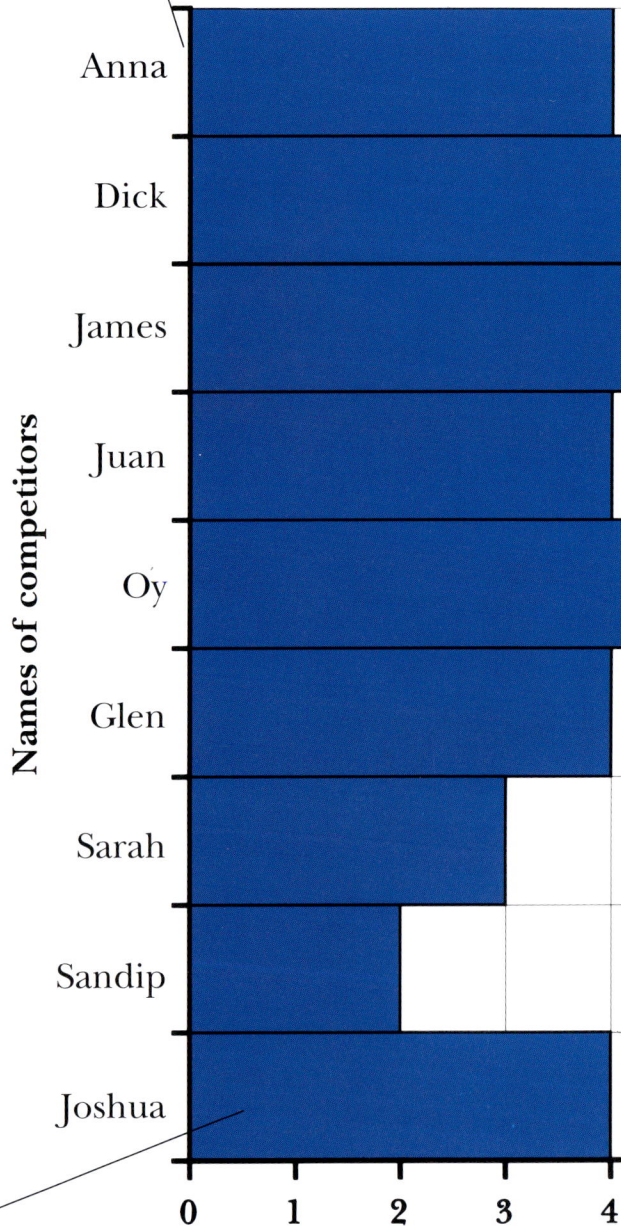

Names of competitors

Anna

Dick

James

Juan

Oy

Glen

Sarah

Sandip

Joshua

0   1   2   3   4

DATA								
Name	Joshua	Sandip	Sarah	Glen	Oy	Juan	James	Dick	Anna
Time (minutes)	4	2	3	4	5	4	10	13	4

3 Each number from the data is now drawn as a bar. If Dick completed the task in thirteen minutes, a bar for Dick is drawn until it reaches the thirteen minutes level on the chart.

4 The columns are then coloured in.

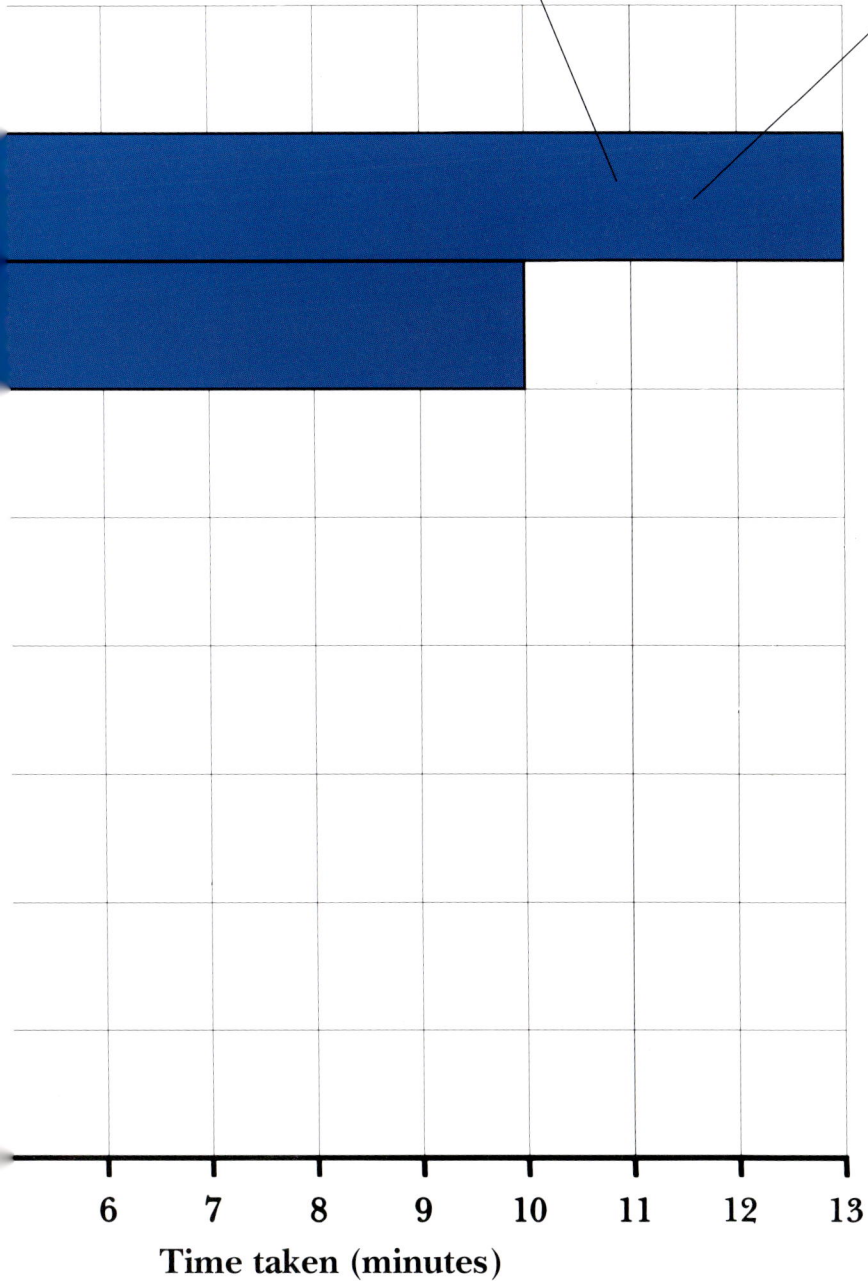

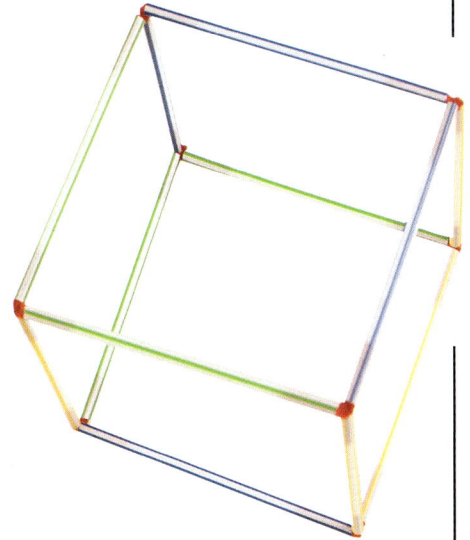

A task such as making a cube from pipe-cleaners and straws can be completed much faster by some people than others. The variation in time can easily be seen on a bar chart such as the one on the left.

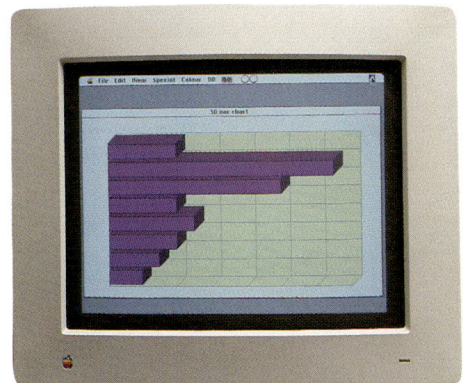

6	7	8	9	10	11	12	13

Time taken (minutes)

A computer-generated 3D bar chart.

Pie charts

A pie chart is useful when you want to show how information adds up to make a whole. For example you may want to show the proportion (**percentage**) of different types of goods that make up a weekly visit to the shops, or the proportions of different types of house in a street.

What data can I use?
To make up a pie chart you need to prepare the data. Your computer can do this for you, but here is how to do it for yourself.

Litter survey
A pie chart can be used to compare the proportions of various categories of rubbish that are collected in a street litter survey.

Use your calculator to complete the table and show that the figures on the pie chart are correct.

1 Write your information down in a column on the left hand side of a page. Then add the information to find the total.

DATA (For litter collection survey)

Category	Number of pieces collected	Proportion of the total(%)	Degrees of a circle (360 degrees make up a full circle)
Steel	4	4/49= 0.08 (8%)	0.08 x 360 = 29 degrees
Tin	2	2/49=0.04 (4%)	0.04 x 360 = 15 degrees
Copper	3	6%	22
Glass	4	8%	29
Aluminium	5	10%	37
Stone	4	8%	?
Plastic	10	20%	?
Paper	13	28%	?
Wood	4	8%	29
Total	49	49/49=1.0 (100%)	1.0 x 360= 360 degrees

2 Work out the proportion of each category by dividing the number of items by the total.

3 Multiply the proportion by 360 to find out the number of degrees of a circle this is equal to.

Wood

Steel

5 Put a label beside each sector.

4 Use a protractor to mark out the circle into sectors.

6 Colour the sectors in.

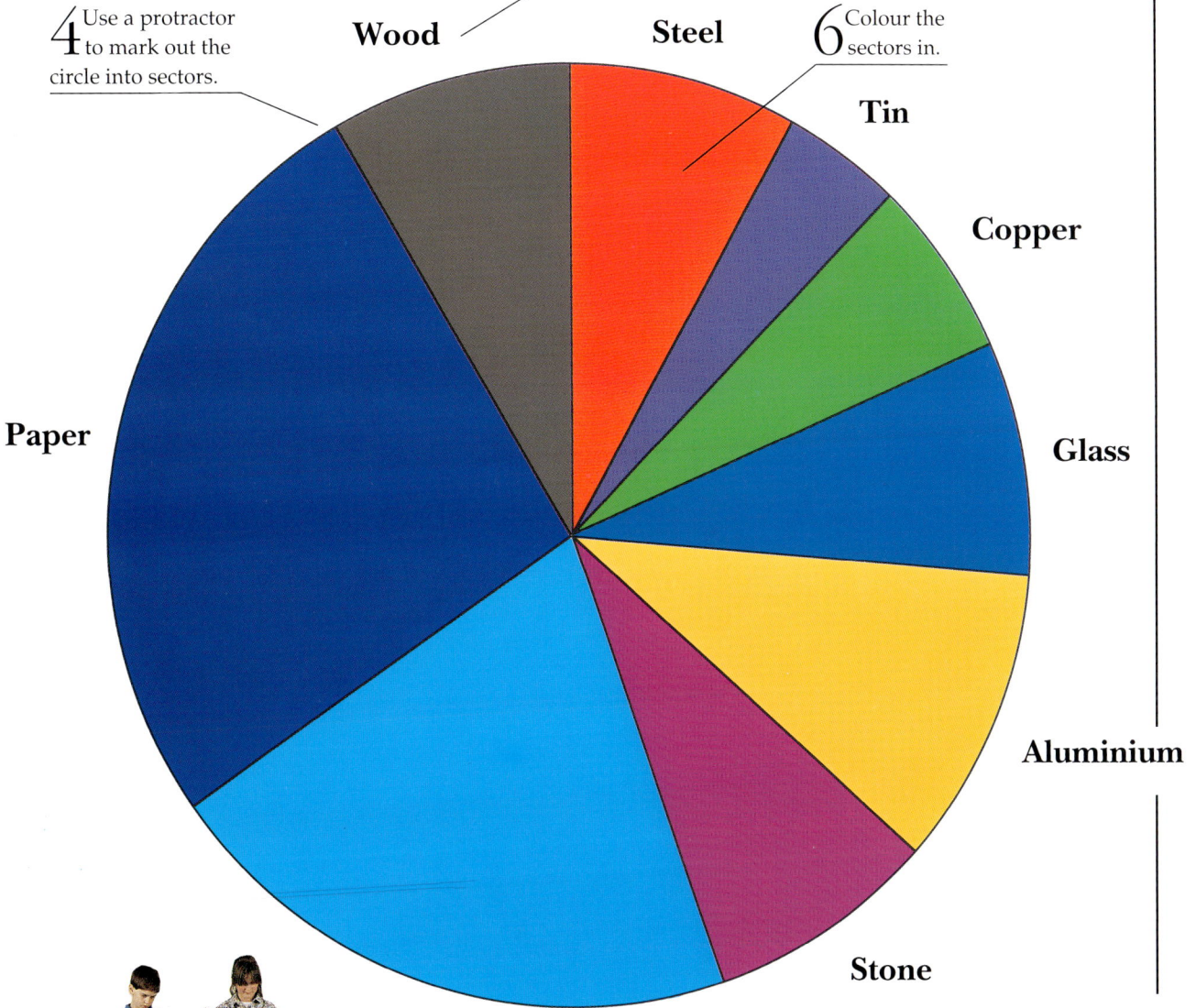

Tin

Copper

Paper

Glass

Aluminium

Stone

Plastic

These people are collecting litter for a street survey. For more information on conservation see the book *Don't throw it away* in the Science in our world series.

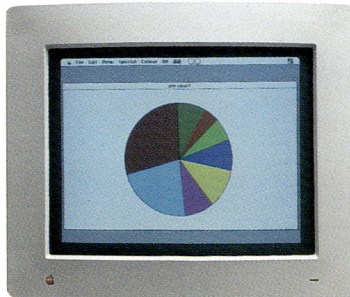

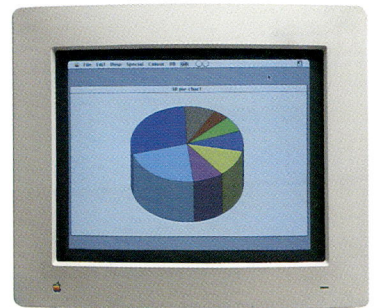

A computer will make pie charts at the touch of a button.

37

Line charts

A line chart is often used to plot the progress of something through time. For example, it might show the cost of a bag of sugar in the shops from week to week, or it might show how far a model aircraft has travelled each second.

Line charts are commonly seen and easy to draw.

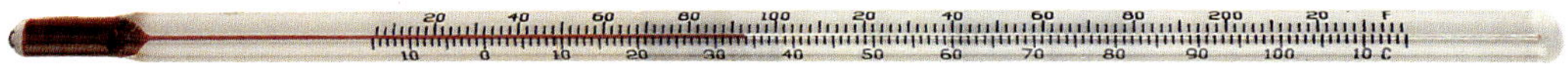

The line chart below shows the way temperature varied over a ten day study period. The temperature was measured at the same time each day.

1 Make a line chart by first drawing two lines (axes) at right angles.

(For more information on temperature see the book Weather *in the Science in our world series.)*

2 Then split each axis into a number of even divisions and add numbers to make a scale. If you are making a speed chart, seconds are set out on the horizontal axis and distance on the vertical axis (scale in m).

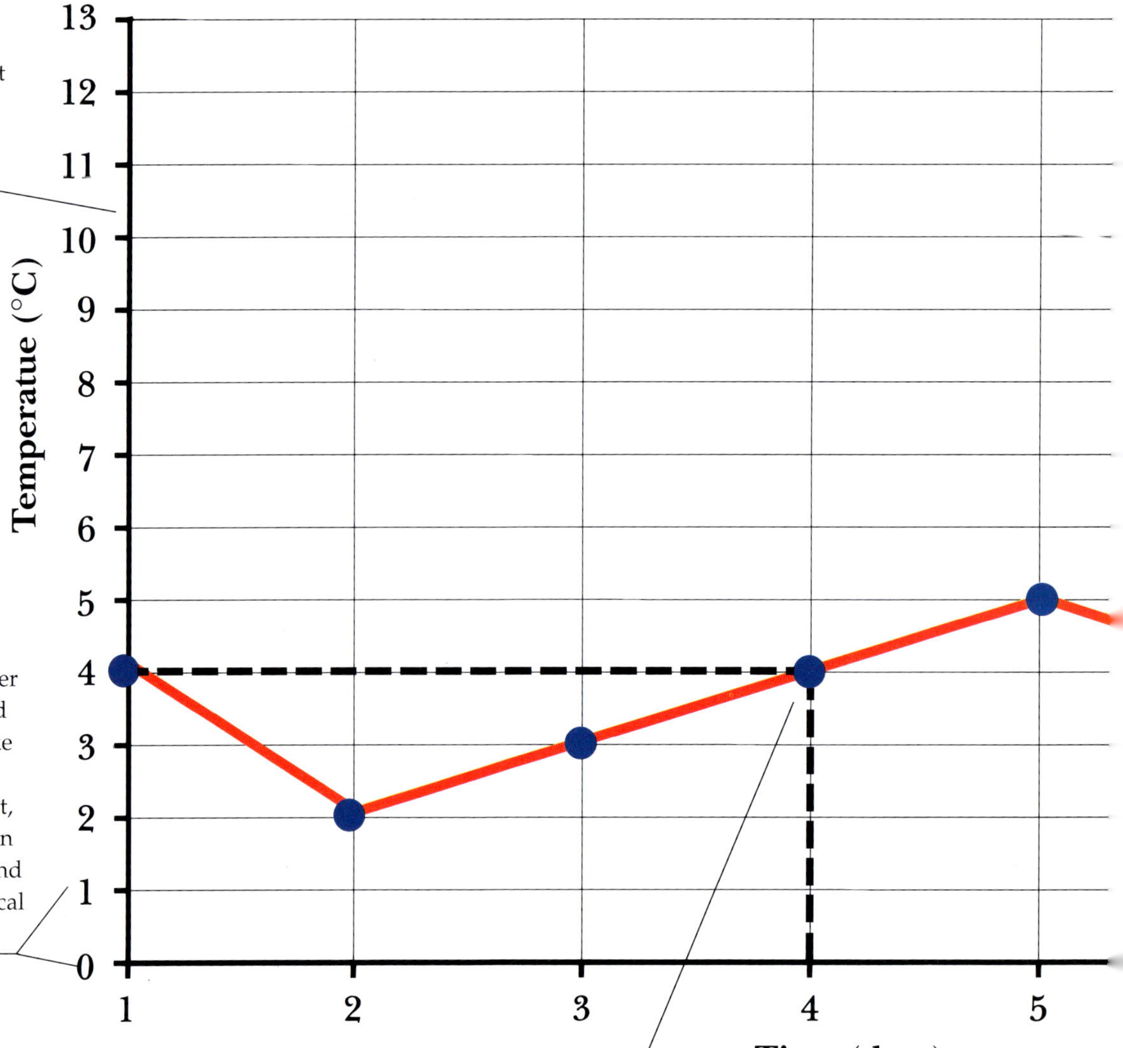

3 Each number from the data is now marked as a circle, a cross or some other symbol. This point shows that, the temperature on day four was 4 °C.

This model is being tested for its acceleration. The time it takes to cover each metre is recorded using a stopwatch. For more information see the book *Starting and stopping* in the Science in our world series.

Heights of people from different age groups in a school can be marked on a line graph to show changes with age. For more information see the book *Growing and changing* and *Science and design* in the Science in our world series.

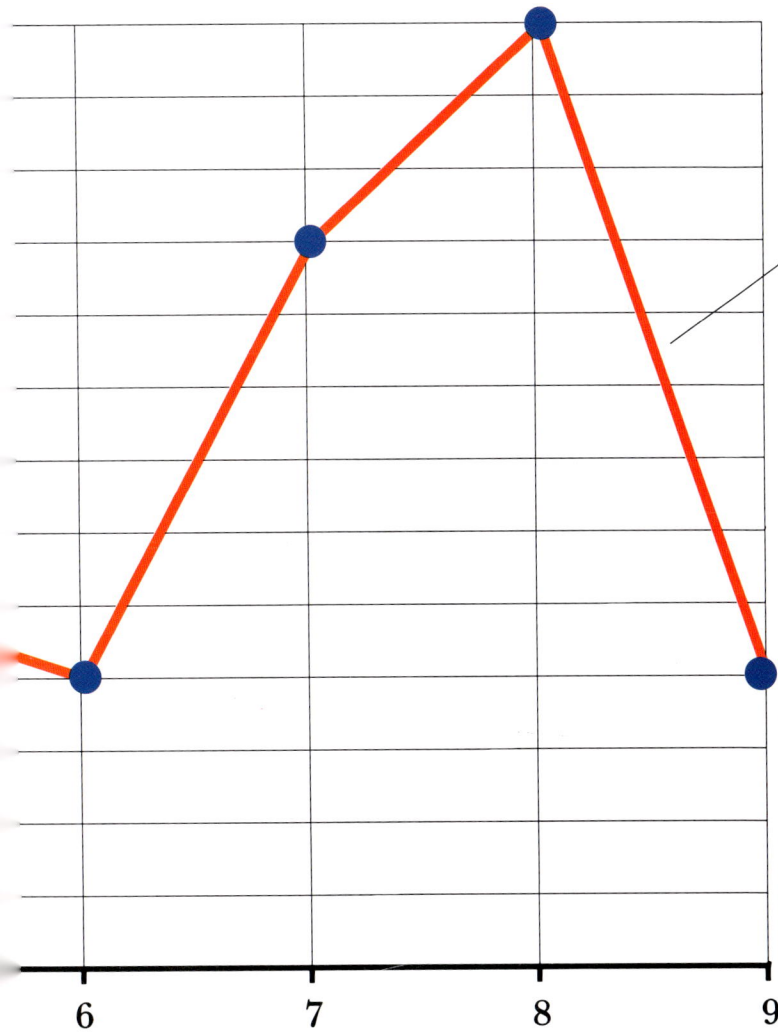

4 The marked symbols are joined by a line.

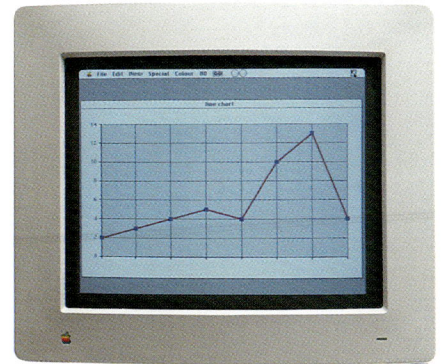

A computer will make line charts at the touch of a button.

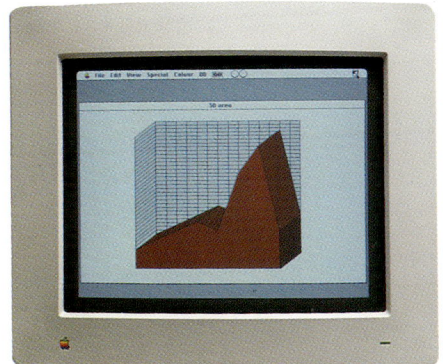

6   7   8   9

Watch your scales!

When you present information you have to be careful to give an accurate impression. Here we show some examples of what happens when the same information is presented with different scales. Some of it can be very misleading!

The two charts below show the same information. Imagine they show, for example, ten computers that have been compared for speed of use.

The top chart appears to show that computer brand eight is way ahead of the others and therefore the one to buy. This is a useful chart for those selling computer brand eight.

In the lower chart the scales have been compressed. Now there appears to be little difference between the computers – a helpful chart for those selling the less speedy computers!

A bar chart showing the heights of the children in the picture below could be used to make either of the following statements: these young children vary in height, or these young children are all about the same height. Which kind of chart scales would make each statement appear true?

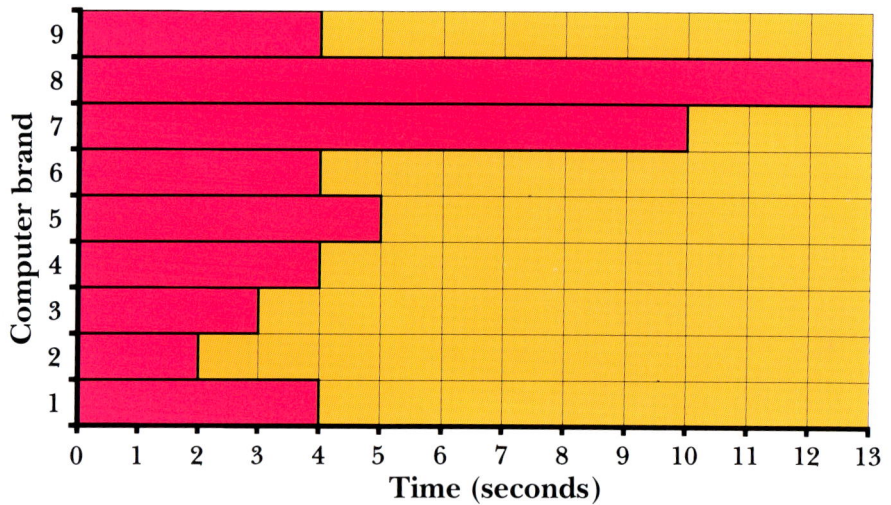

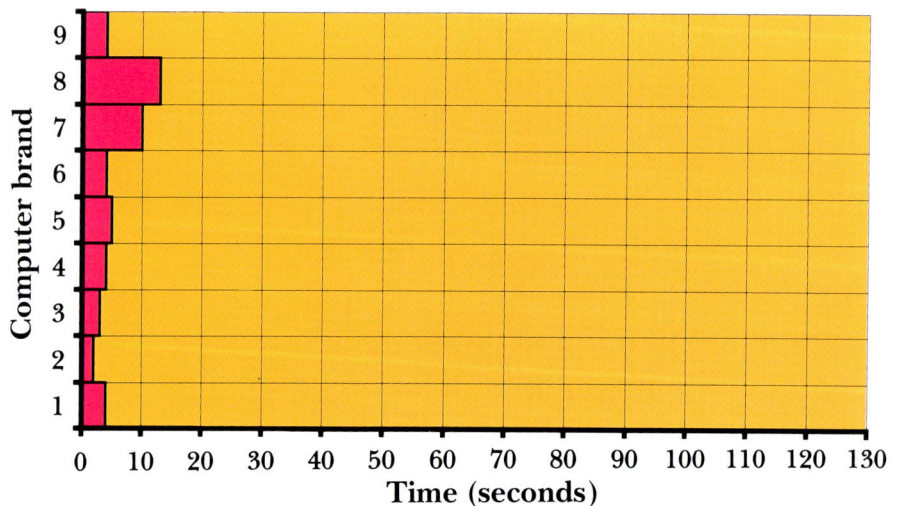

The two charts below show pollution levels in a city measured in milligrams of pollution in each litre of river water. In the top one it seems that at the end of month 7 there was a high level of pollution. However, in the lower chart the same information is shown but the scale has been changed so that the maximum value is 1000. Now it appears that pollution is hardly ever a problem at all!

The heights of people in a class can be plotted using either of the chart types shown on these pages. But the charts also show how careful you have to be to make sure that the scales help people to understand the information correctly. For more information on measuring heights see the book *Growing and changing* in the Science in our world series.

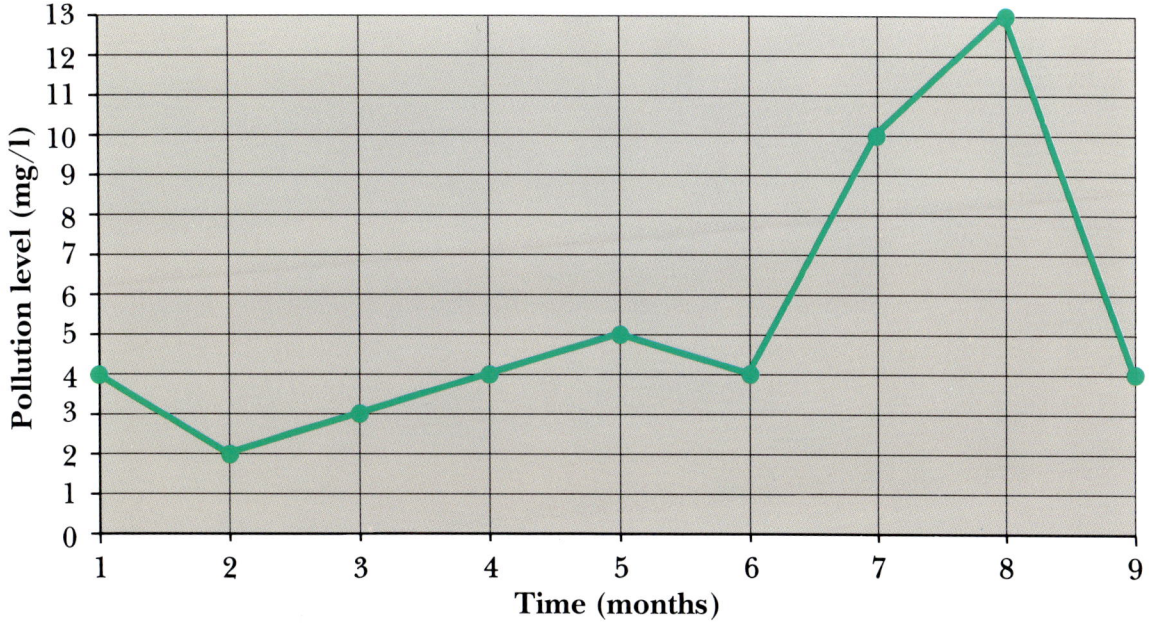

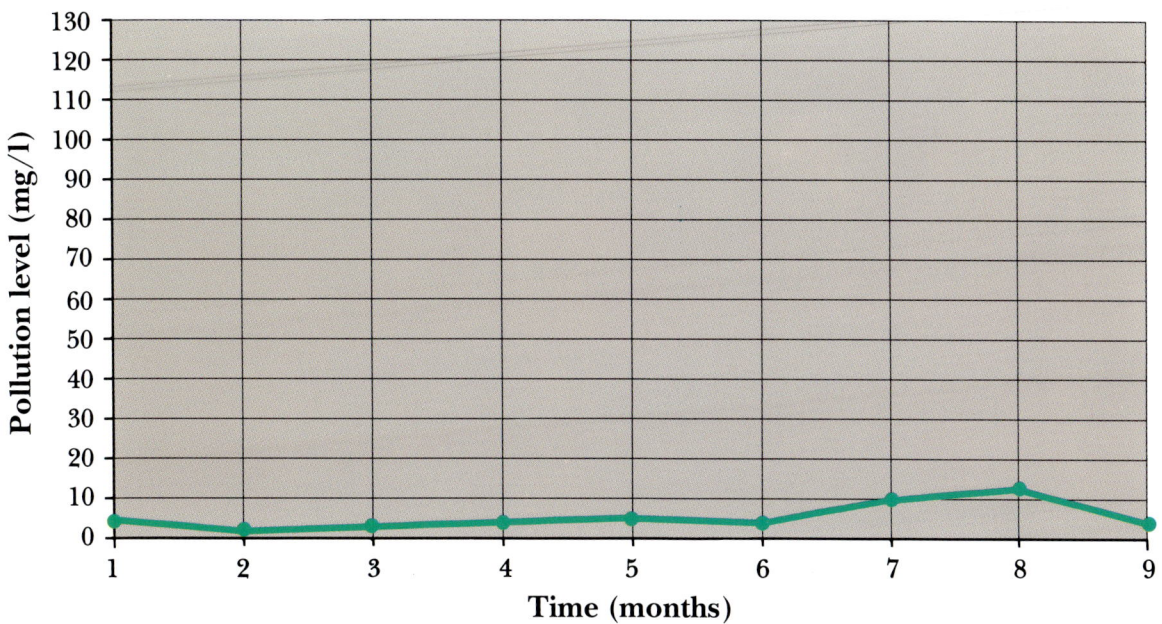

Flow charts

A flow chart shows the order in which something happens. In an experiment there may be many steps to follow and it is helpful to show these in a form similar to the one on this page.

There are many other times when you might want to use a flow chart, for example, when setting out information with many alternatives and links, such as a computer program or a family tree.

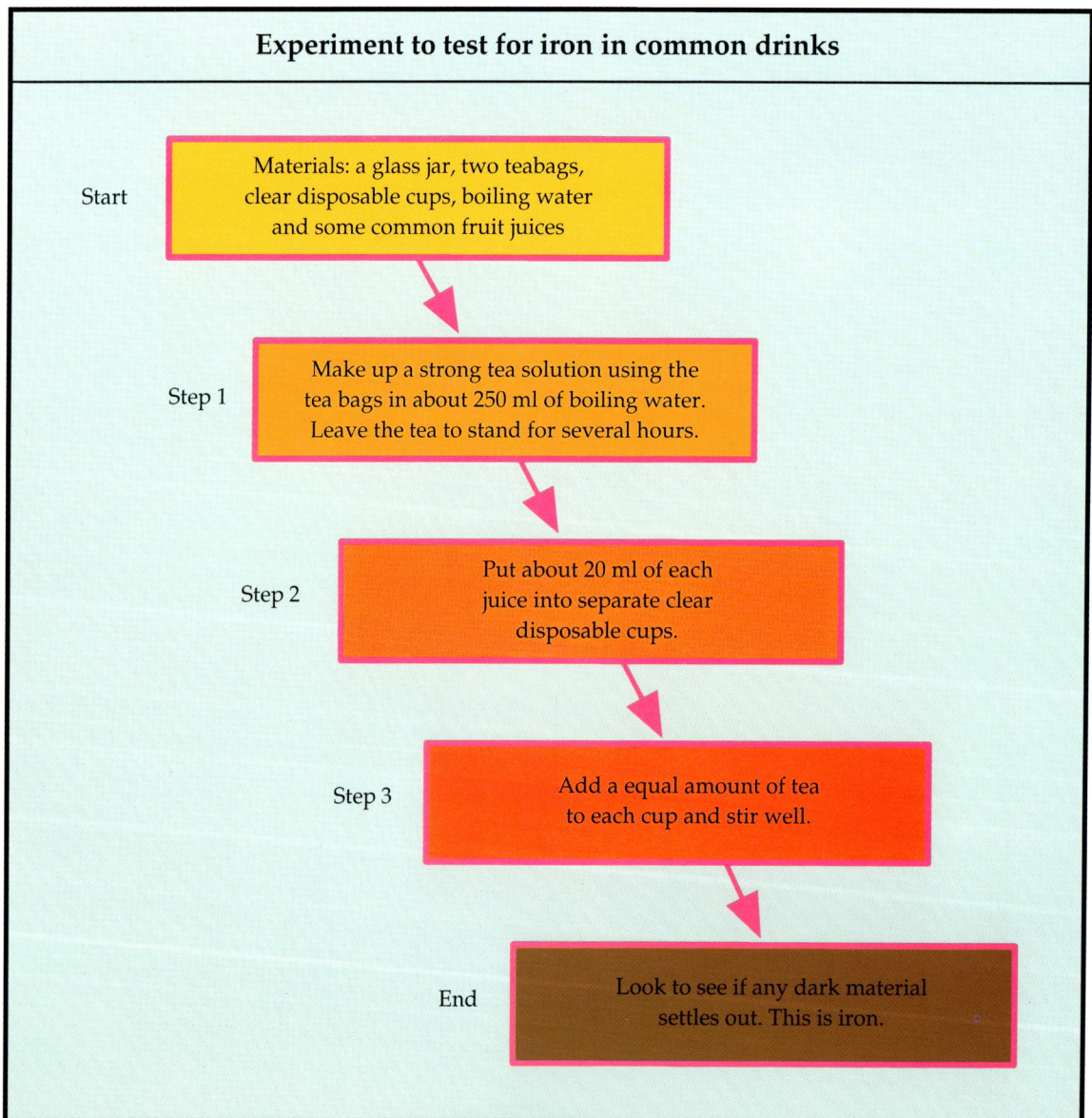

Experiment to test for iron in common drinks

Start
> Materials: a glass jar, two teabags, clear disposable cups, boiling water and some common fruit juices

Step 1
> Make up a strong tea solution using the tea bags in about 250 ml of boiling water. Leave the tea to stand for several hours.

Step 2
> Put about 20 ml of each juice into separate clear disposable cups.

Step 3
> Add a equal amount of tea to each cup and stir well.

End
> Look to see if any dark material settles out. This is iron.

Dissolved carbon dioxide in rainwater.

Carbon dioxide enters the atmosphere from volcanic eruptions.

Carbon dioxide is given off when fossil fuels are burned.

Animals breathe out carbon dioxide.

Green plants convert carbon dioxide in the atmosphere into living tissues.

Dissolved carbon dioxide in sea water.

Animals eat plants.

Limestone is eroded and carbon enters sea water.

Plants and animals die and the carbon enters the soil.

Some carbon is locked up in rocks as limestone or as fossil fuels.

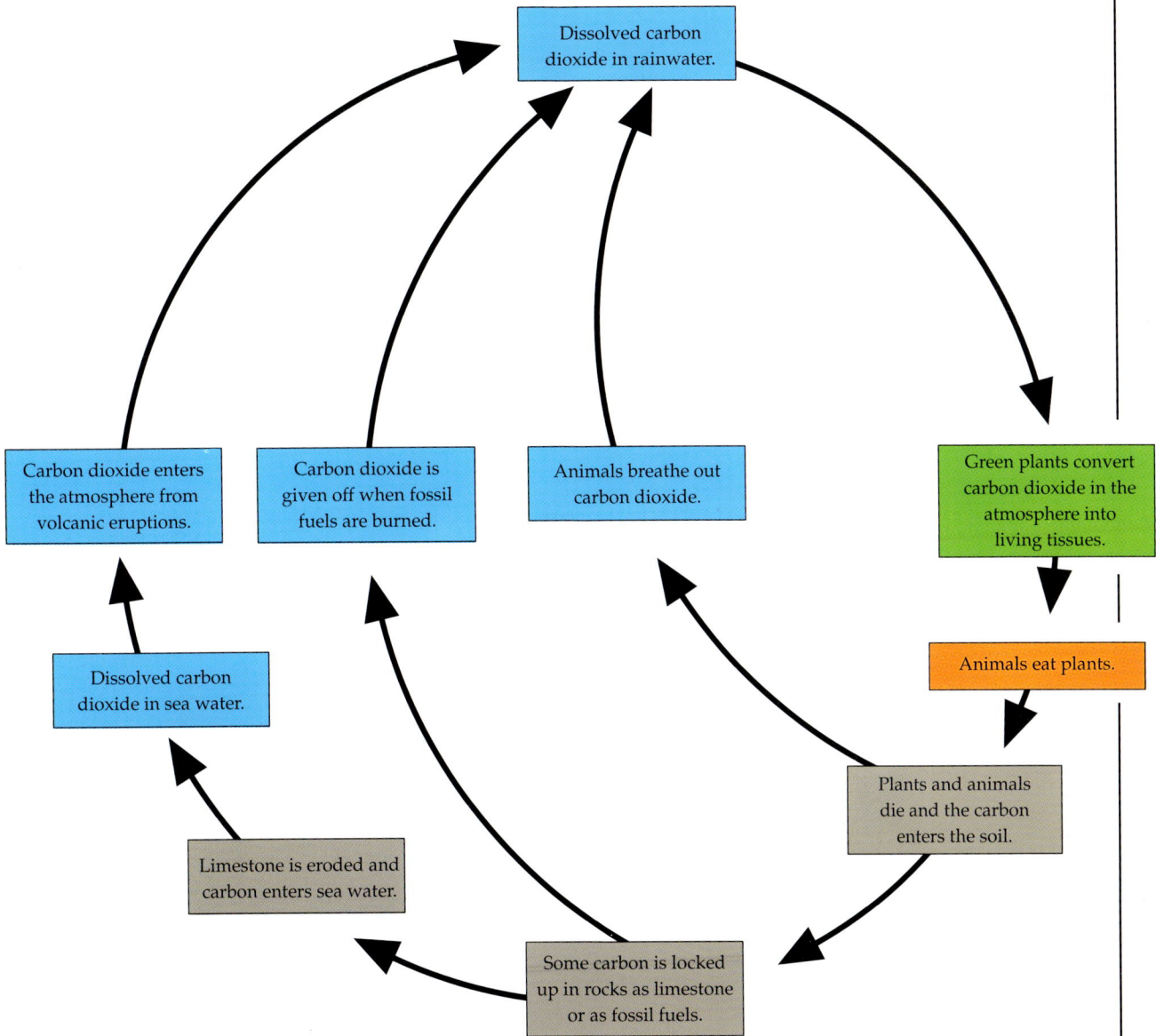

Circular flow charts

The **carbon** cycle is an example of a circular flow chart. The lines connect up the main parts of the cycle. Each important store of carbon is drawn as a box containing detailed information. The way the carbon moves on Earth is shown by arrows.

By making the information fit into a simple chart it is much easier to understand even very complicated ideas such as the carbon cycle.

(For more examples of flow charts wee the book Water *and* How the Earth works *in the Science in our world series.)*

Your family tree

A family tree is a chart of all your relations, traced back in time. It flows from the top (the oldest ancestors) to the bottom (yourself).

Make up your own family tree.

(For more information on the way family trees are drawn see the book Time *in the Science in our world series.)*

Using illustrations

Many books are accompanied by photographs and drawings. These illustrations are there to provide additional information that would not be easy to desribe in writing.

Each type of illustration has to be matched to its purpose. Compare, for example, the illustrations in school books and magazines and you will find that they are very differently presented. Here are some guidelines on how illustrations can be presented for school work.

This is a map of the world's major vegetation zones.

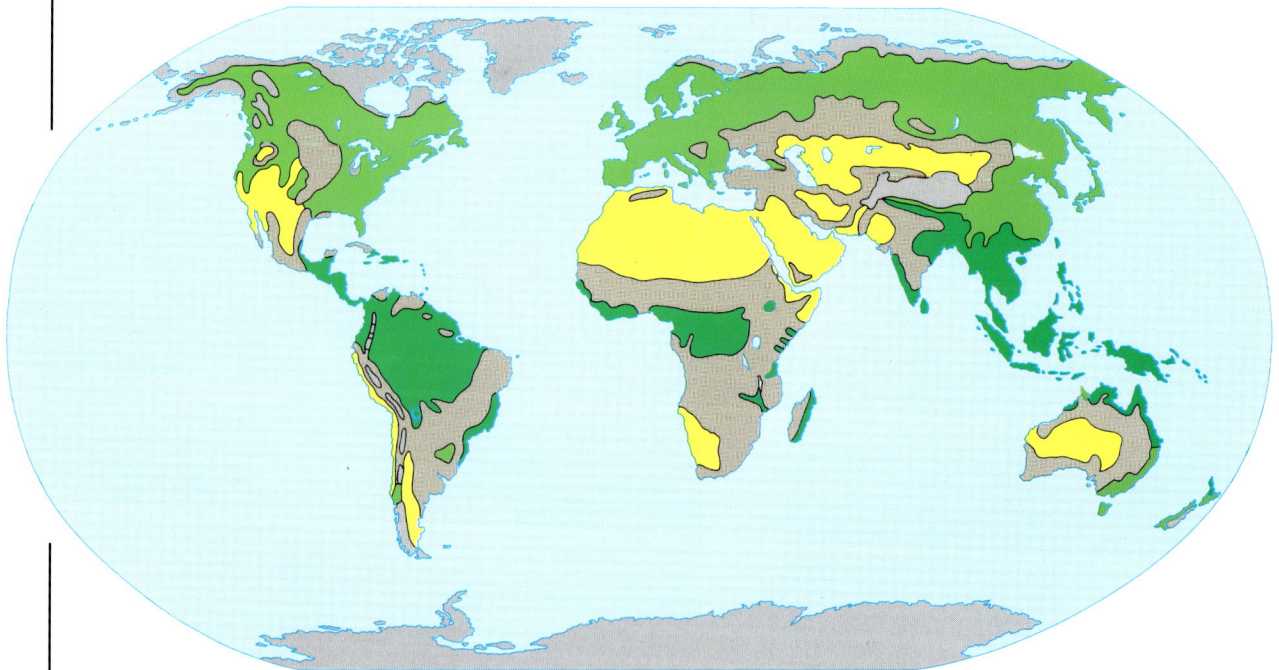

■ Temperate forests, with cool winter	■ Grasslands, where rainfall is sparse	■ Deserts, where rainfall is very sparse	■ Tropical forests warm all year

Maps
Maps are extremely useful for showing the distribution of data within or between countries. For example a map can show the number of cases of a disease in countries, or the distribution of earthquakes or vegetation throughout the world.

A colour key provides extra information. However, colours must be chosen with care. Blue always suggests water, for example, whereas brown or red are denser colours and therefore suggest a greater value than a light colour such as yellow.

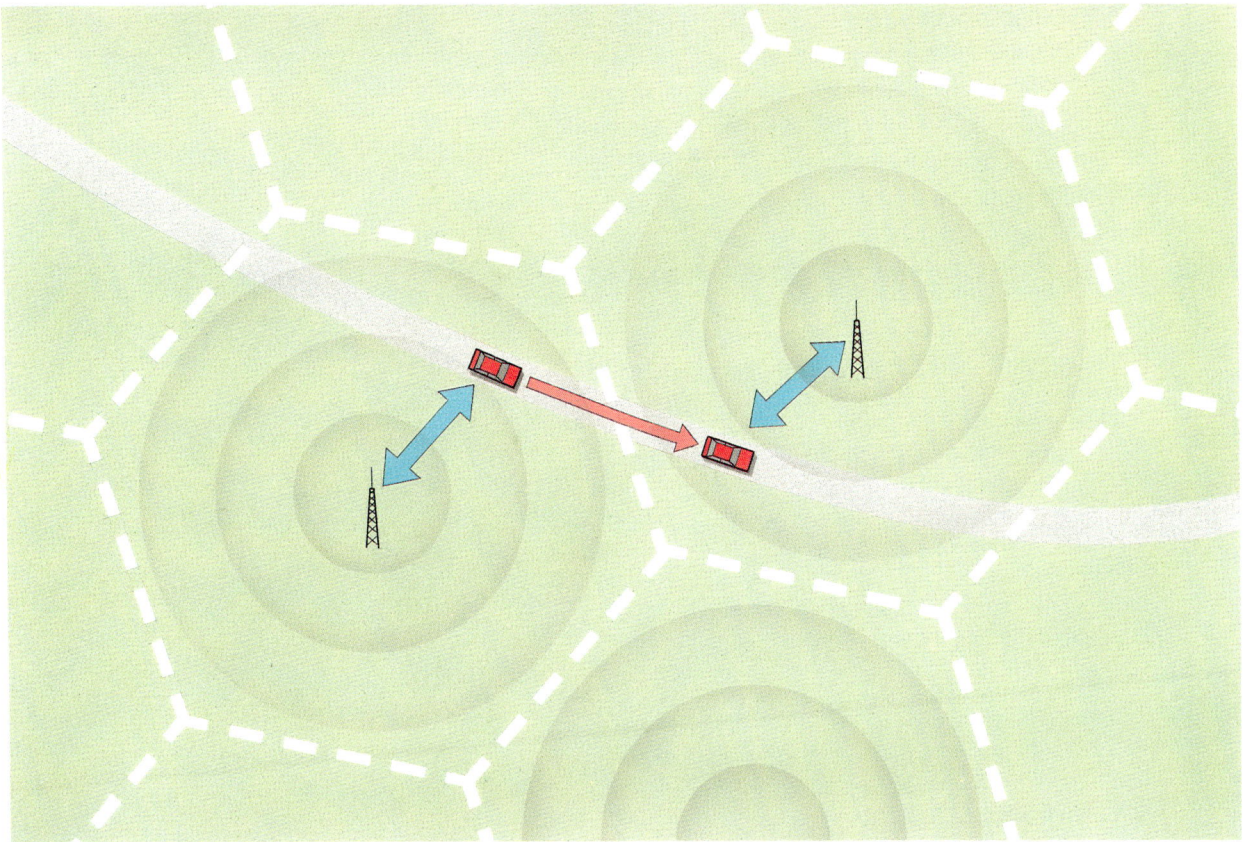

Graphics

The type of illustration shown above (called a graphic) is commonly found in a newspaper or magazine. Its job is to illustrate a subject that may be completely new to the reader. This one shows what happens when a driver using a mobile telephone travels through a honeycomb network of transmitters.

Cross-sections

This type of illustration is often used to show how a solid object works. In this case a cross-section has been taken through the centre of the head.

Cross-sections are explained by using labels. The line connecting the label to the corresponding place on the cross-section is called a leader line.

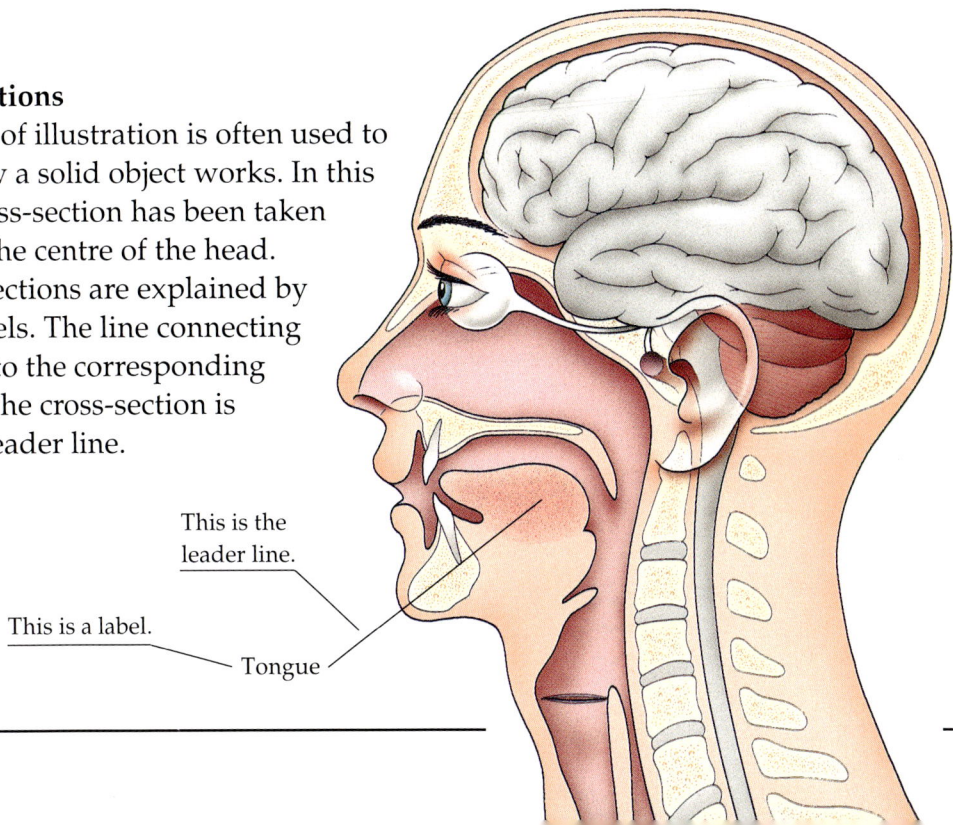

This is the leader line.

This is a label. —————— Tongue

New words

axis (axes)

when drawing a chart the horizontal and vertical reference lines are called axes. The place where the axes join is called the origin of the axes and its value is usually zero. Scales are marked along each axis from the origin

carbon

one of the basic elements, or basic substances, which are the building blocks of everything in the Universe. Carbon is an essential element for life. Of the 11 billion substances known, 10 billion of them contain carbon

colour blindness

a term which refers to the difficulty some people have in recognising certain colours, especially red blue-violet or green. Colour blindness is an inherited disorder and it is mostly found in males

communicate

the many ways in which meaning is sent or understood from some information. The word is used in many ways: it is used to describe a conversation between people, exchanging data between computers and the courting actions of animals

data

a series of observations or measurements that have been collected as part of an experiment or investigation. Another common word for data is information

designer

a person who works out the shape and structure of something using sketches, computers and other aids

dimensions

a measurement of the size of something in a particular direction such as length or height. In drawings the three dimensions are mass, length and time

field of view

the total region that a person can see. In people the field of view is made up of the field from the left eye and the right eye. Together they make a more or less oval field of view, with a 'blind area' just in front of the nose

focus

the region that can be seen clearly and where all objects appear to have sharp outlines. Special muscles within the eye pull the lens into different shape so that we can focus on objects at different distances

illusion

something which deceives the brain by giving a false impression. There are many illusions which are used to advantage: for example a mirror gives the illusion that the images seen in the mirror are as far behind it as the real objects are in front

image

a representation of an object. In relation to eyes and lenses an image is the representation of the object that is brought into focus on the back of the eye

lens (of eye)
the small flexible disc of transparent material in the front of the eye. The lens is responsible for making light rays focus on the back of the eye

long-sighted
a disorder of the eye which means that the muscles cannot pull the lens far enough for a person to be able to see short distances clearly. This disorder is corrected by the use of contact lenses or spectacles

magnetic disks
circles of material, usually plastic or aluminium, which have a coating of fine iron particles and which are used in computers to store information. Disks that are shared between computers are often called floppy disks

optical discs
a circle of rigid material such as plastic in which there is a pattern of tiny pits. Optical discs are often known as compact discs or CDs

percentage
the value of something when expressed as a proportion of hundredths. Thus a half is 50 hundredths or 50 percent and a quarter is 25/100 or 25 percent. The symbol % is often used instead of the word percentage

pictographs
a representation of a word or group of words made in the form of pictures. Many ancient pictographs were made on the walls of caves. The most widely used pictographs today are the Chinese and Japanese characters used for their written language

scan
to glance over quickly. The word is used in computing to mean a machine that sweeps across some information, gathering the data and making it available on a screen

short-sighted
a disorder of the eye which means that the muscles cannot pull the lens far enough for a person to be able to see long distances clearly. This disorder is corrected by the use of contact lenses and spectacles

technologist
A person who makes use of scientific discoveries to make goods which can be used. For example, the existence and nature of radio waves was discovered by scientists, but technologists then made use of this natural property to make radio sets that we can all use

transmitter
a mechanism that is able to send out information. Our vocal chords are a form of transmitter because they send out sound waves which can be detected (heard) by other people

Index